PRINCIPLES
OF LOVING
ONE-ANOTHER
RELATIONSHIPS

Discipling
REDEFINED

Editor
CHRIS CARTER

Discipling Redefined
Principles of Loving One-Another Relationships

© 2020 by Christopher Carter

Printed in the United States of America
ISBN: 978-1-948450-96-6.

Unless otherwise indicated, all Scripture references are from the *Holy Bible*, New International Version, copyright 1973, 1978, 1984 by the International Bible Society. Used by permission of Zondervan Bible Publishers.

Illumination Publishers titles may be purchased in bulk for classroom instruction, teaching seminars, or sales promotional use. For information, please email paul.ipibooks@me.com.

Illumination Publishers cares deeply about using renewable resources and uses recycled paper whenever possible.

Book interior layout: Toney C. Mulhollan.

Cover design by Roy Appalsamy of Toronto, Canada.

About the Editor: Christopher Carter, became a disciple almost twenty years ago. He is passionate about helping people become more Christlike. He promotes mentoring relationships in his work at Lexus HQ and as an adjunct professor at Georgia Tech. He and his wife, Michelle, and their children, Mason, Naomi and Noelle make their home in Frisco, Texas.

www.ipibooks.com
6010 Pinecreek Ridge Court
Spring, Texas 77379-2513, USA

dis·ci·pl·ing
/dəˈsīpəlNG/

noun
- the process of one becoming more and more like Christ via loving one-another relationships

verb
- helping one another to become more and more like Christ

adjective
- describing a relationship where two or more are striving to become more and more like Christ

Table of Contents

Acknowledgments

Thanks and praise to our Lord Jesus and to the Father, who has put his perfect plan into action in our lives so that we could become his disciples. Thank you, Lord, for showing us the prime example that we should follow! I pray we can take up your attitude in our hearts.

Much gratitude is owed to my dear wife, who not only deals with all my craziness, but also is a great mother to our three children. Without her support during the year of this book's creation, much of the inspiration and the required time to undertake this project would not have been possible. Thank you, Michelle, for allowing me to contribute to this work! I love you.

There's too much to say about my mom and dad. I owe them my life. They have instilled in me a sense of hard work, respect for others, and the value of family. I will always hold my parents in high regard. I love you, Mom and Dad. Thank you!

Big thanks to my two closest mentors, who have poured into my spiritual development in many ways over the past four years. They have given me much input and advice, and lent to me their wisdom on how to serve in this capacity. Thank you, Derik Vett, and thank you, Gordon Ferguson!

I'd be remiss not to communicate how deeply indebted I am to some of my closest friends in various churches who contributed to coauthoring this book with me. They have spent hours upon hours meeting, discussing, praying, debating, and considering how to best approach this tough topic. I am super thankful for all of you! Thank you, Nate, Nafiisah, Omar, Alex, and Joi!

—Chris Carter

Foreword

Maybe you are like me. I am not much interested in a long foreword in a book. I am usually ready to get right into the meat of the subject written by the authors themselves. So let me just briefly commend this book to you.

I was raised in a church environment where there was a lot of talk about "restoring New Testament Christianity." The idea made sense: through the years, believers had wandered further and further away from the teachings of the Scriptures, and what this led to was something far away from the original plans to follow Jesus. What was needed, it was said, was to get back to New Testament Christianity.

However, as I considered the movement that came from this effort, what I discovered was that something much like the proverbial elephant in the living room was there in plain sight. You could be in the movement for years and hear lots of teaching on various subjects but never hear anything about the nature of relationships among disciples and how critical they are to the whole Jesus enterprise.

Some things that were never intended to be a pattern for all time were taught as strict requirements by imposing on the Scriptures a questionable hermeneutic (or type of interpretation). At the same time something like disciples' relationships with one another, that hardly needed a specialized hermeneutic, were thought of as secondary topics or ignored altogether. With this approach, it was possible to have the church be like a hollow shell, where on the outside things looked quite biblical, but on the inside was missing the essential nature of the church as well as the way our relationships are to affect the growth and development of heart and character.

Sometime in the early 1970s many of us noticed that there are a great many places in the Scriptures that include the term "one another." When we looked closer, we saw that in most every reference we were being told something vital about qualities that were to be in our new relationships. These were qualities that would help us grow and be examples of God's new kingdom breaking into this world.

To be a Christian was to be a disciple of Jesus, and these passages were showing us how "to disciple" each other to Jesus. Over the last nearly fifty years several of us, who are now getting a little long in the tooth, have written books on this subject, as we saw a great resurgence of interest in this vital need. Not surprisingly, this led to exciting growth and change. But from time to time, groups and movements drift away from the principles that contributed to their vitality. It happened or was in danger of happening in New Testament times (e.g., Galatians 1:6–7; Hebrews 2:1–3; Revelation 2:1–5). It still happens today. It happens to us.

In view of this, it was with joy that I learned of the work being done on the book you are about to read. Here you have material that was envisioned, planned, and developed by the next generation after my own. They are the age of my children. You are going to hear from some new voices who have seen for themselves what the Scriptures teach about our need to connect deeply and significantly with each other if we are to seriously follow Jesus.

Editor Chris Carter and his cowriters have put together a most needed volume that takes a fresh look at the "one another" concept, and then gives us some useful tools to help us bring it to life through the Spirit's power. As one who has been seeking transformation through relationships for decades, I am thankful for these younger ones who can help me see how to take new steps forward. God works through relationships. He has in store more than guys like me have known, and I say, "Bring it on."

So read carefully and put into practice what you hear. I commend it to you.

—Tom A. Jones
Nashville, Tennessee

❶

WHY REDEFINE?

It was just before the Passover Festival. Jesus knew that the hour had come for him to leave this world and go to the Father. Having loved his own who were in the world, he now showed them the full extent of his love.

—John 13:1 NIV1984

Prior to going to the cross, our Lord decided to have a meal with those closest to him. As Jesus entered this moment, he was focused on showing his love. The Lord would go on to establish an example and teaching about relationship for the Twelve that would serve as the staple for generations of his future followers to continue to draw upon. He called it a **new command.** He said by following it, the whole world could come to know about him. Sounds like something decent enough to write a book about... So here we are, staring at some of the modern church's deepest issues and coming back to this point in time.

The Need to Redefine
An alarming trend has been observed that churches are no longer reaching the youth and families in their communities and are drastically slowing in growth. The data confirms it. It's happening in our churches all over America, and in other countries as well. Have

you seen it? Have you felt it?

Often observed is a decline in deep and genuine relationships, a lack of devotion to the body and generally there is a negative connotation associated with accountability. In some churches, terms such as:

- Discipling
- "D-Time"
- "Discipler"

…and the like have such a negative meaning that some have abandoned the biblical practice altogether, except in name only. Of course, the terms are not sacred, but the heart behind them is very much so for the body of Christ.

Recently a small group of diverse sisters and brothers in the faith have been inspired to work together to counter this negative connotation and prayerfully stir hearts back toward well-rounded sound doctrine from our Lord Jesus, centered on: "A new command I give you: **love one another**" (John 13:34).

Many, many sermons, lessons and books on the topic of discipleship have been based on John 13:34–35, and the aim for this book is not to forget those classics, but to build on the foundation they have laid and redefine, or in some cases remind each other about, the sound doctrine that accompanies loving one another.

So now the obvious question comes to mind: *how should we practice loving one another?*

A New Command

Taking flight from Jesus in John 13, he shows to the Twelve what is called "the full extent of his love" (NIV1984). You may know the story well. He washes their feet. He makes time to humble himself and take the place of a servant in a personal act of servitude, in which Jesus literally washes the dirt off grown men's feet. I imagine what I would feel if I were one of the Twelve… Maybe I'd think to myself, wow, this guy is really doing me a favor since my feet are in bad shape! He is really taking care of me by doing this, and in fact I can't believe how patient he is getting my pinky toenail so clean! Now that

I think about it, I really trust this guy. I wouldn't just allow anyone to touch my feet like that.

Perhaps Jesus wanted the Twelve to feel OK with him doing this for them, as he asks, "Do you understand what I'm doing for you?" He wants them to feel safe and secure, not only in this physical act, but ultimately for the salvation of their very souls. He shows them this real love, and afterward gives a brief yet mind-blowing lesson that concludes with this NEW COMMAND:

> *"Love one another. By this all people will know that you are my disciples"* (John 13:35 HCSB).

How many of us would consider this a "discipling moment" or a "d-time"? Is this what discipling can look like? Perhaps it could, since this scripture is referenced quite a bit on the topic. Just consider what these twelve did after they spent this time with Jesus... One of these guys debated Jesus, only later to preach a gospel sermon to thousands on the day of Pentecost. Another became known as the "apostle of love." Several went on to become elders and pillars for the first-century church. And that early group of disciples spent quite a bit of time together, serving one another, taking care of each other, and growing more Christlike with one another. I guess they followed this new command. They took loving one another seriously enough to strive to live it out to the best of their ability.

Let's Redefine

How many of us who have been living faithfully for quite a while now would define a "discipling time" as one in which much of the time spent with one another was focused on serving each other? Or taking care of each other's needs? Or better yet, a time of having each other's backs, enhancing our trust in one another? Surprised? But maybe these are the countless examples found in Scripture that are the raw, uncut, pure forms of discipling.

You have heard that to be a disciple means to be a follower, learner, or even apprentice of someone, some concept, or some skill. OK, let's start with that. So in our case (as disciples of Christ), we want to be like Christ. If it was basketball, be like Mike, right? If kung fu, I'd

figure be like Bruce Lee. If Street Fighter, be like Ryu's Hadouken...
for you younger readers. If we start with being like Christ, 1 John 2
states that we must walk as he did. So what did Jesus prioritize? What
are the key things one must do to walk as he did? Better yet, what are
the deal-breakers for being his disciple?

The Bible explicitly calls out at least two key items: to be his
disciple:

1. **You have to love your brother and sister, and**

2. **You have to be willing to deny self.**

I'd sum it up this way: we have to help each other be like
Christ primarily through loving each other and helping each other
repent. What were his priorities? Pretty sure love is near the top, but
specifically loving each other in very many ways... Also repentance
and forgiveness would obviously be high on the list. And seeking and
saving the lost has got to be in there, right? We must help each other
become like him in these ways.

Let's refresh our minds and hearts about it. At its root, discipling
is about *relationship*. It's about how we relate to one another, given
we all want to be more Christlike, and given we all just want to
make it to heaven. I think it really can be that simple. God gave us
a great example in Jesus. If we take a good, long look at Jesus as he
"discipled" (even though he never used the term), maybe we will be
surprised at what we see. What "new" thing can we find together?
What "new" thing is right under our noses? Or maybe we will stumble
upon something old we forgot about.

Quick Disclaimer

Timeout. Before we execute a rather deep and insightful dive
into redefining the practice, let's take a moment to clarify what our
aim is with this book, and what it is not. Our aim is not to discredit
the positive practices of the past, nor is the aim to act as if we haven't
made mistakes and learned some valuable lessons. It is fruitless to
spend alot of time "beating on the past" here.

The goal we are praying for is to produce in every reader's heart:

- A *Refined focus* inspired from God's word
- A *Refreshed hope* for those looking to the future
- A *Reviving healing* for those hurt by the past
- A *Redefined conviction* to love one another
- A *Renewed desire to* imitate Christ

The intention of the redefining exercise in these chapters is for us to reengage—like reengaging muscles that have become weak. Those muscles can feel so heavy! But we take one step at a time, and slowly the muscle begins to ACTIVATE and grow strong.

A Simple Exercise

♪ Won't you be my neighbor?♪, sang Mr. Rogers. I grew up on that. So here goes my best imitation: Won't you join me in an exercise? It's a simple exercise to search and find together the biblical realities we can glean from. Let's look first at Jesus, then at other examples from both Testaments. I'm sure we can find together plenty of practical examples of loving one-another relationships—the kind that produce the type of fruit we all long for.

To help us in our exercise, we've invited a diverse group of brothers and sisters, all from different walks of life, to help guide us as coauthors. Think of this group as the exercise-video instructors, who are sweating hard and trying to perfect the routine for the viewers working out in the comfort of their own homes. They want to be examples of what being in great shape is all about! Normally, I can't stand those folks, with their ripped abs and perfect form… Well, take a breath, none of us are that perfect—ha ha! But I deeply respect each member in this group of coauthors who will be sharing their own convictions and life experiences. I'm sure you will be able to relate to at least a couple of us. No pressure.

We intend to write this book taking broad stokes from the past, but diving deep into convictions we believe are worthy to **HOLD ON TO.** When was the last time you heard a sermon or teaching about trusting one another? Have you read a chapter in a book lately talking about protecting one another? Has it been a long time? Again, the muscle activates. Remember, *the muscle is there.* I mean, it's not a new muscle; it's always been there. Perhaps we just need to build it back up. There will be soreness and fatigue, but we must keep exercising it. In just fourteen days (says the uber-fit trainer), you will feel brand new and be on your way, enjoying your new strength.

If You Build It...

What happens when we focus solely on results? We all want to see people converted to Christ, baptized in the water, openly confessing sin, and repenting like crazy, right? I believe we all want this ideal state in the church. So why does it seem so hard?

I believe Jesus wants us to focus on building the process or building the culture. Then he comes and makes it happen ("by this all people will know..."). So what kind of process leads to the result described? Is it not the process of love? You know that second greatest command, or the one that all the Law and Prophets or whatever commandment there may be hangs on. OK, super answer there alright, but let's break that down a bit. How is love realized in the church? Is it not via love being expressed in various forms within our relationships? So is the answer found in loving one-another relationships? That seems so indirect.

Let's build one case. Say a conviction to make others feel protected begins to grow. It becomes such a focus that the level of trust for one another in the church is on the rise. Pretty soon the church feels to the everyday member like a safe and secure environment, where everyone has your back for real. What happens when you feel most secure with one another? You let your walls down and become more vulnerable. It's the classic case between two good friends. They talk about it all—the good, the bad, and the ugly. Maybe if we build this kind of culture, God will bless it and make it fruitful. The kind of fruit that lasts, leading to the results of widespread confession of sin and repentance as a majority culture. Just one case, if we build it.

The Devil Is in the Details

Our enemy doesn't like the sound of all this, by the way. The temptation to think love is too hard, or the thought, Why look at that old dusty stuff again? may pass through the mind. That's the devil. The common issues we have observed, like complacency in small groups, secret sin, lack of openness, decline in church growth, or even challenges to raise up new leaders, do indeed have similar roots. It's a bit detailed, like how love is a bit detailed. Complacency's enemy is *perseverance.* Sin's enemy is *forgiveness.* Stagnant evangelism's enemy is *hope.* Pride's enemy is *patience.* Hurt's enemy is *kindness.* Doubt's enemy is *trust.* Spiritual failure's enemy is *love.* Love never fails. Satan knows this, so of course he works very hard to hide it from us even though it is in plain sight.

Love Never Fails

I believe in the power of love, and the power found in loving one-another relationships. We may not be able to sprinkle magic fairy dust on the church with this book and overnight solve all these common issues, but we at least want to stir hearts and minds to *try.* Love will not fail us. Perhaps if we redefine discipling in this light, we can continue to grow closer to each other and closer to our Lord. Let's be willing to open our minds to both the old and the new as we redefine the Royal Law, redefine overcoming sin, and redefine the discipling relationship.

Let's go.

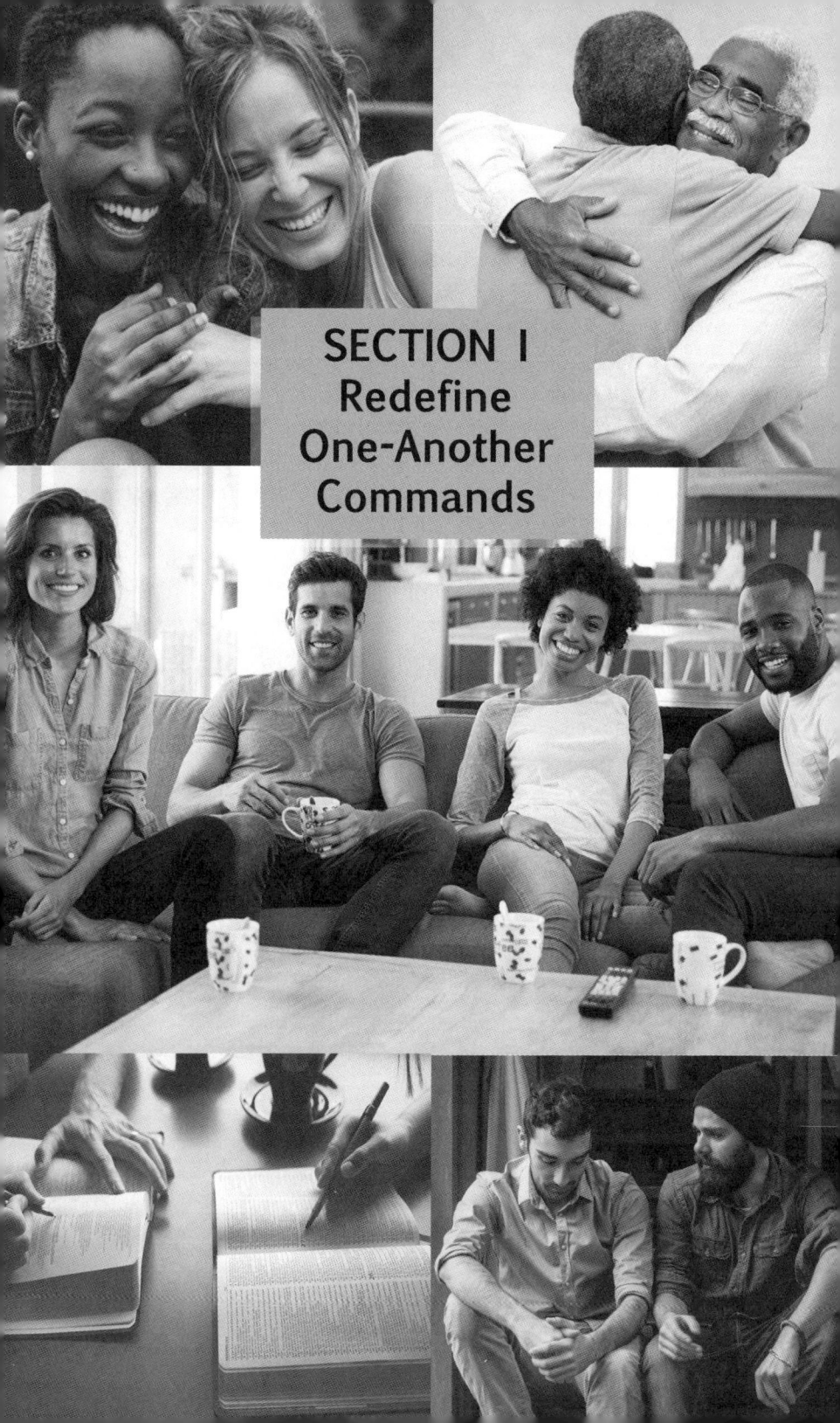

SECTION 1
Redefine One-Another Commands

2

A Relationship Full of Patience

As a prisoner for the Lord, then, I urge you to live a life worthy of the calling you have received. Be completely humble and gentle; be patient, bearing with one another in love.

—Ephesians 4:1–2

A relationship without patience is like a car with little to no gas. You are not going to get far.

That's why I wanted to invite my friend and sister in Christ, Joi Freeman, to share some insights about the value of patience in our one-another relationships. She will also share some cautions for us all to consider about how impatience can hurt our relationships. Let's look at the following perspective and consider how we can grow in doing unto others as we would have them do unto us.

_____ **Coauthor Introduction: Joi Freeman** _____

Joi is a strategist by trade who has spent most of her career playing matchmaker between brands and consumers. She was converted in Chicago in 2007 as a young professional. Joi has worked with the teen ministry, led in the young professionals ministry, and now serves as a mentor helping emerging leaders discover and cultivate their unique gifting. Joi is a frequent contributing writer, speaker, and presenter on topics including Millennial and Gen Z culture, how to integrate faith and work, the impact of changing cultural and racial demographics, and the role of women in the secular world and faith community.

The Race of Patience

"My only aim is to finish the race and complete the task the Lord Jesus has given me—the task of testifying to the good news of God's grace" (Acts 20:24).

Imagine running in a marathon. You finally decided to tick running a race off your bucket list. Today is the big day. Over 15,000 people are running. Though the weather is scorching and humid (not ideal running weather), the atmosphere is exhilarating with the music, large crowds, and eager runners ready to take off.

You are not the elite runner. You are not the midlevel runner. You are the novice. You are in the back section of the last wave released to run, yet you leave the gate with great anticipation. Unfortunately, around mile fourteen you hit the wall. Your muscles are weak, you feel fatigued, and a sharp pain pierces your shins. You are literally running on empty. You question why you even registered for this race, whether you are capable, and if all your training was worth it. As you survey the near-empty road you question whether you have the strength to finish.

So why keep going? At mile eighteen you're greeted by lively volunteers at the water station screaming "Ice cold water!" They eagerly pass you cups of refreshing water that you didn't realize you desperately needed to rehydrate on this abnormally humid day. The sprinkling of spectators who committed to staying to see the last runner shout, "You can do it!" "Pace yourself but don't give up!" And as you hit that wall, their passionate encouragement keeps you going. Their willingness to remain on the sidelines until you have passed, with an eagerness displayed to elite runners, sparks something deep inside you to push through your wall, your physical limitations. With the support of the volunteers serving you and the spectators cheering for you, you finish the race!

The race is much like our lives, spiritual journeys, and discipling relationships. We play one if not multiple roles at any given point in our spiritual journey.

patience (noun)

pa•tience/ˈpāSHəns/

- the capacity to accept or tolerate delay, trouble, or suffering without getting angry or upset

Patience is the runner who does not give up. During the difficult path along the marathon, they remember the example and advice of their trainer and endure pain and exhaustion to finish the race. Yet patience is also the volunteer at the water station. Patience is the coach who runs alongside their athlete giving them supportive instructions to help them endure until the end. It is the spectator who decides to stay until the very end to cheer for a complete stranger, the novice athlete running alone and struggling to finish. The news cameras are gone, most of the crowd has left, and the event crew is packing up the tables, yet these people stick with it and cheer with the same eager anticipation for the last runner staggering along the road as they had for the elite marathoner whose graceful stride has long passed the finish line.

These people's commitment is not driven by the runner's performance—their speed, form, or level of fitness. This small crowd endures on the sidelines for hours in the scorching sun and thick humidity because they believe every runner needs refreshing water and encouragement to finish the race.

What does it look like to embody the character of patience in discipling?

With tender humility and quiet patience, always demonstrate gentleness and generous love toward one another, especially toward those who may try your patience (Ephesians 4:2 TPT).

Stooping Down to Pour Olive Oil and Wine

> *The religious scholar answered, "It states, 'You must love the Lord God with all your heart, all your passion, all your energy, and your every thought. And you must love your neighbor as well as you love yourself'"* (Luke 10:27 TPT).

In an overscheduled, results-oriented, device-saturated, emoji-communicating world, do we really have the patience to love our neighbors as well as we love ourselves? Is our world saturated with so many filters that we have lost the ability to truly see one another?

> *Jesus replied, "Listen and I will tell you. There was once a Jewish man traveling from Jerusalem to Jericho when bandits robbed him along the way. They beat him severely, stripped him naked, and left him half dead.*
> *"Soon, a Jewish priest walking down the same road came upon the wounded man. Seeing him from a distance, the priest crossed to the other side of the road and walked right past him, not turning to help him one bit.*
> *"Later, a religious man, a Levite, came walking down the same road and likewise crossed to the other side to pass by the wounded man without stopping to help him.*
> *"Finally, another man, a Samaritan, came upon the bleeding man and was moved with tender compassion for him"* (Luke 10:30–33 TPT).

How often are we, in our discipling relationships, one of these four characters in the Parable of the Good Samaritan? How easy it is to be the people of God, living fully religious lives that are empty of the patient willingness to be inconvenienced and to sacrifice for one another. Without the capacity to endure, our discipling relationships can be absent of the compassion that caused the least religious person to see a stranger's pain, bind the wounds, and carry them to a safe place to recover.

In 1973 two Princeton University social psychologists, John Darley and Daniel Batson, tested the Good Samaritan concept in an experiment later published in their paper entitled "From Jerusalem to Jericho." In short, the experiment explored what influences our helping behavior. Darley and Batson recruited seminary students for what they thought was a talk about vocation. Half the students were individually instructed to prepare a five-minute speech about their work in ministry and the other half were asked to incorporate the Parable of the Good Samaritan into their talk. Each was then individually sent to a different building on the other side of campus to give their talk and provided with varying time limits to get to the other side of the campus. The researchers planted an actor pretending to be in distress along each student's route.

What the students did not know was that this was the real assignment. To assess who stopped, they were scored on a scale ranging from failing to notice the person at all, to stopping and asking if they needed help, to stopping and refusing to leave the person's side or insisting on taking the victim somewhere. The result: the preassigned focus—talking about vocation or the parable—seemed to have little impact on which group stopped. The greatest driver for the seminary students to help the person in distress was *time*. The students on a tighter deadline where less likely to notice the helpless person or less likely to stay by their side.

> "He [the Samaritan] *stooped down and gave him first aid, pouring olive oil on his wounds, disinfecting them with wine, and bandaging them to stop the bleeding. Lifting him up, he placed him on his own donkey and brought him to an inn"* (Luke 10:34 TPT).

The Princeton experiment highlights how our rushed lives can put us in opposition to the compassion of the Good Samaritan in Jesus' parable. While we do not know the motives of the priest or the Levite, we do know that the Samaritan was willing to see the beaten and near-dead Jewish man. He came down to his level and then sacrificed his resources to sooth and disinfect his wounds. The Samaritan decided to carry the man when he couldn't walk and get him to a safe place where he could recover. If patience is the tireless long-suffering to endure with a good temper whatever comes, then Jesus gives us a blueprint for patience in discipling relationships in the actions of the Samaritan.

Take Two Scriptures and Call Me in the Morning

In the absence of patience, our one-another relationships can become one-another transactions—a collection of exchanges that feels like you are receiving a spiritual prescription to fill at the kingdom pharmacy.

- Have you ever received input that had absolutely nothing to do with the problem you shared?

- Have you ever shared your heart only to get the sense that you were not being heard?

- Have you ever used one of these phrases as a workaround for not knowing what to say? "I'll pray for you," "Did you pray about it?" or "God gives you the desires of your heart."

Much like using CTRL+V (or CMD+V for my fellow Mac users) we can create shortcuts in discipling relationships, which allows us to copy and paste biblical principles, questions, and responses that do not require us to truly invest. In essence, our gospel-centered one-another relationships become one-another transactions that allow us to easily pull prepackaged biblical concepts off the shelves of our mental inventory. When a situation arises, we simply unbox, warm, and serve regardless of the actual spiritual nourishment required in that situation.

Yet imagine if Jesus had a CTRL+V approach to ministry and discipling. The advantage is that he could have been incredibly efficient. I mean, think about his conversation with the Samaritan woman in John 4. It took nineteen verses for him to reveal he was the Messiah. And it took thirty-four versus before she was productive in her evangelism. With a little CTRL+V, we could have arrived at these conclusions a lot earlier and with fewer words.

"I have no husband," she said.
"That's nicely put: 'I have no husband.' You've had five husbands, and the man you're living with now isn't even your husband. You spoke the truth there, sure enough" (John 4:17–18 MSG).

Jesus already knew her situation before she even spoke! So why waste time drawing out her life story, talking about water, and hinting as to the Messiah? Jesus had already turned water into wine. This moment at the well with all this water would have been a perfect time to copy and paste one of his miracles to speed up her realization. Maybe he didn't because Jesus is not a transactional Lord. His time with the woman at the well was about <u>more than her having knowledge that led her to change.</u> It was an opportunity for this Samaritan woman to experience the character of Jesus in a way that would inspire transformation.

Now, many Samaritans from that city believed in him and trusted him [as Savior] because of what the woman said when she testified, "He told me all the things that I have done." So when the Samaritans came to Jesus, they asked him to remain with them; and he stayed there two days. Many more believed in him [with a deep, abiding trust] because of his word [his personal message to them]; and they told the woman, "We no longer believe just because of what you said; for [now] we have heard him for ourselves and know [with confident assurance] that this one is truly the Savior of [all] the world" (John 4:39–42 AMP).

<u>Without experiencing a relationship with Jesus, would she have had a personal testimony</u> to share? If Jesus had merely transacted with her, what would she have testified to the Samaritans? And if she did, would it be recited knowledge or an unwavering belief?

In his time with the Samaritan woman at the well, Jesus shows us what it looks like to patiently unveil the truth. To ask the questions of one another even when we are positive we know the answers.

Some Things to Consider

1. Would your friends, family, and sisters and brothers in the church consider you to be patient?

2. Do you ask questions and listen to others?

3. Do you draw people out versus offering quick fixes?

4. Considering that patience is a command, not a suggestion, how could you improve upon patience as a part of your practical repentance?

3

A Relationship Promoting Humility

Therefore if you have any encouragement from being united with Christ, if any comfort from his love, if any common sharing in the Spirit, if any tenderness and compassion, then make my joy complete by being like-minded, having the same love, being one in spirit and of one mind. Do nothing out of selfish ambition or vain conceit. Rather, in humility value others above yourselves, not looking to your own interests but each of you to the interests of the others.

In your relationships with one another, have the same mindset as Christ Jesus. —Philippians 2:1–5

Please consider the words of one of my favorite authors, C.S. Lewis, as he describes meeting a humble man in *Mere Christianity*:

> Do not imagine that if you meet a really humble man he will be what most people call "humble" nowadays: he will not be a sort of greasy, smarmy person, who is always telling you that, of course, he is nobody.

Probably all you will think about him is that he seemed a cheerful, intelligent chap who took a real interest in what you said to him.

If you do dislike him it will be because you feel a little envious of anyone who seems to enjoy life so easily. He will not be thinking about humility: he will not be thinking about himself at all.

Selfless love. Love that is kind, love that is patient, that is neither boastful nor selfish. These are the things that promote humility in our relationships. When I was in college at Georgia Tech many moons ago, I observed this type of kindness in a good friend, my sister in Christ, Nafiisah Renshaw. She will share some key elements about how we can cultivate our relationships with the kindness that shows we truly value one another.

Coauthor Introduction: Nafiisah Renshaw

 Nafiisah grew up in the ICOC churches as the youngest child of a woman who became a disciple in 1987. She was baptized in 1997 as a teenager in Atlanta, and her journey as a disciple has been filled with struggles and blessings. She has experienced and been in the mentoring role of discipling relationships that were deeply relational, and others that were more like weekly or biweekly meetings. Looking back, Nafiisah can confidently say that she learned from all her former disciplers but will always feel a connection to the ones that went beyond "checklist discipling" (i.e., Did you read your Bible? Did you pray? What sin do you need to confess this week?) to share their hearts and lives and connect with hers. That is why she felt drawn to contribute to this important project. Teaching, correcting, and admonishing one another is, at its core, about relationships.

Take Two Scriptures and Call Me in the Morning

As Joi shared, we must be patient with one another as we call each other higher. Coupled with patience is kindness. A person cannot be truly kind if they're not patient, and vice versa.

According to Merriam-Webster.com, the adjective "kind" is

defined as "of a sympathetic or helpful nature; of a forbearing nature: gentle; arising from or characterized by sympathy or forbearance." Would the people you disciple, officially or otherwise, describe you as sympathetic, helpful, gentle, and trustworthy?

Would they say things like:

- YOUR NAME HERE: _____
  is nonjudgmental when I confess my sins and struggles. She/he gives me advice and counsel based on Scripture and biblical principles, not her/his own opinions. I can tell she/he really wants to help me be like Christ.

- She/he asks questions to draw me out and shows me Scripture to help me repent of my sins. She/he helps me have a godly perspective of my daily life and habits.

- She/he doesn't respond harshly if I don't follow her/his advice. I know she/he is focused on my obeying Scripture, not her/his counsel.

- She/he is great at not gossiping about my struggles. I am confident that our conversations are confidential.

If you aren't quite sure, then ask them, but be humble and listen carefully to their responses.

Run Your Race and Help Them Run Theirs

The Scriptures call us to be disciples of Jesus Christ, not disciples of each other. Yes, it is advisable to imitate each other as we imitate Christ (1 Corinthians 11:1), but ultimately we're disciples of Christ, not of one another. Each one of us is in an individual relationship with God, and that relationship is as unique as the disciple in it. We certainly have a lot of commonalities; we share similar struggles, for instance, but we each have our own spiritual race to run (Hebrews 12:1–3).

Each path, each walk is unique, but there are common roadblocks. It says in 1 Peter that the devil is like a roaring lion looking for someone to devour; just after that it talks about knowing that others, your brothers and sisters around the world, are also going through the same struggles (1 Peter 5:8–11). No one is alone in this. Our struggles may be at different points in our lives, a roadblock may look slightly different from one person to another, but they are similar, so we can help one another.

As we teach and direct one another, we can share the things we've learned when we've experienced like challenges. What has helped us overcome our spiritual battles? It's important, however, to remember that what worked for us might not work for the person we're seeking to help. Let's not judge others for "failing" in areas where we tend to "succeed." The source of such judgment is pride, not kindness (Romans 14). Instead, we ought to humbly impart the wisdom God has blessed us with, and trust God to move in their hearts and work in their minds to guide them to what they should do. It is far greater to nurture someone through a struggle toward working out their own salvation with fear and trembling (Philippians 2:12–13) than to condemn them for their weakness (Galatians 5:14–15).

Bear With One Another

We are called to clothe ourselves with a heart of kindness and bear with each other (Colossians 3:12–13). We certainly shouldn't excuse sin! Jesus never did, so neither should we, but let's help people celebrate small victories and set goals for incremental change; because repentance is really a mind change, not a behavioral change (2 Corinthians 7:8–12). For many people what happens first is the behavioral change, but if you just rely on a change in habits, then there's not true repentance. The result will be sinning repeatedly in the exact same way (Acts 8:9–24). As we help one another get to heaven, we need to help each other have the mind shift, the perspective shift, the biblical focus shift that is necessary and more lasting than a new "good" habit. But that takes more time, it takes a lot of patience and kindness, and it takes a lot of perseverance. It takes repeated discussions about the same concept, the same struggle, the same topic for there to be true victory.

There are sins that are sometimes described as "pet sins," the things that are ingrained in us, in our sinful nature, that we will deal with to varying degrees for all our lives. We'll have victories over it in our current situation, but in a new situation that's to come tomorrow or a year from now, we'll struggle again. Take confidence in the knowledge that a fruit of repentance is knowing what to do to be victorious if you ever find yourself in the exact same battle you once fought. There will be new challenges, and you'll have to continue to work on that same sin. Acknowledge that while celebrating the small victories, and rejoice in the repentance that has happened. Celebrate the changes that are going on and know that there will always be more. Don't be discouraged by that fact, because you know that you're growing along the way; you are becoming more and more like Christ (2 Corinthians 4:8–18).

Advice Is Just Advice

Something that is commonly forgotten or ignored is that advice is just that, advice. It is unwise to completely ignore advice (Proverbs 12:15), but our thoughts, opinions, musings, or what have you are not the word of God. In discipling relationships we ought to be humble and do our best to help each other with counsel that is rooted in Scripture, knowing that our advice is only advice and that the person may choose to follow it or not, and that the counsel we give may be good or it may be horrible.

That's right, I said it…horrible. Don't be so proud as to think that your advice is always great or infallible (1 Corinthians 3:18–20). We give advice, counsel, guidance, et cetera through the lens of our own experiences and perspective. What we're saying may be in line with God's will and guidance, or something entirely different. We don't necessarily know the quality of our advice, but we can trust that counsel rooted in Scripture is a tool used by God to guide the person on the receiving end to his will (Isaiah 55:10–11). Trust that the person is going to be led to all truth and righteousness by God (John 16:12–14), and help them be confident of that as well. God will take care of them. Discipling is not about you.

Helping someone be a better disciple, be more like Christ, more holy, more complete, not lacking in anything (James 1:2–4) is not about us, the advisor, discipler, or leader. It's not about us saying the right things, in just the right way, at just the right time. If anything, it's about us being a humble instrument of noble purpose through which God can communicate his love, his wisdom, his way, his righteousness, his mercy, his forgiveness, his greatness, his awesomeness to someone. We are just tools (2 Timothy 2:20–26). God willing, tools for noble purposes, but we're tools. We're only the ones planting seeds, watering, and harvesting (1 Corinthians 3:5–7). We are not the One who makes anything grow; we are not the One who brings about repentance; we are not the One who brings about a heart change. *God is the One who does that.*

It's our job to listen to the Spirit, to pray with people, to kindly guide them to Scripture, and to help them see God when they're most challenged and when things are going great.

Avoid Gossiping

How well can people trust you not to mention to someone else what's shared with you in confidence? In other words, do you avoid gossiping? At times we are trying to help someone and we need help ourselves in order to figure out what type of advice to give when we're confronted with a situation where we lack experience, discernment, or wisdom to think of a scripture that applies. We seek advice from people who are, ideally, wiser and biblically grounded, but often our conversations turn into gossip and not truly seeking advice. We end up just having a conversation about someone but not necessarily getting the help that we need to help that person.

The habit of leaving a person's name out when seeking advice for them is something I do as often as possible. That habit is not a direct command or instruction found in the Bible. Scripture doesn't say "don't mention someone's name when you're seeking advice," but it speaks about not gossiping (Proverbs 20:19) and not betraying confidences (Proverbs 11:13). I've found that leaving people's names out when I'm getting guidance on how to help them is a practical way to avoid gossip and slander (Romans 1:29–32; Ephesians 4:29–32).

Circling Back

Back to the question I asked at first: "Would the people you disciple, officially or otherwise, describe you as sympathetic, helpful, gentle, and trustworthy?" What do you think now?

Some Things to Consider

1. Would your friends, family, and brothers and sisters in the church consider you to be warm, inviting, loving, and kind?

2. Are you humble enough to offer God's word prior to offering your advice?

3. Considering that both kindness and humility are commands, not suggestions, how could you improve upon these qualities as a part of your practical repentance?

A Relationship with Mutual Respect

Be devoted to one another in love.
Honor one another above yourselves.

—Romans 12:10

A relationship without proper respect is doomed to cause deep hurt that could lead to utter disunity, and at its worst, possibly create an enemy. This is a serious topic, an area where we must develop deep conviction to build the community of Christ.

One of my best friends, Nate Bigbee, will lead us in some thoughts considering how we must hold each other in high regard. I love and respect this brother. He takes us through some of the do's and don'ts in our one-another relationships that we should pay close attention to.

_____ **Coauthor Introduction: Nathan Bigbee** _____

Nathan Bigbee is an evangelist at the Mission Point Christian Church in San Antonio, Texas. He and his wife, Waldina, lead the South region of the church and the young professionals ministry. They serve on the Singles Service Team and oversee the singles throughout the states of Texas, Louisiana, and Oklahoma. Nathan also works with the singles leaders on the continent of Africa.

Hurt Will Happen

Over the years I've seen a lot of amazing as well as bad practices when it comes to helping others be like Jesus. We are all sinners, we will all hurt one another, and we will all be hurt by others. That's a fact you can take to the bank. We are sinners hurting and helping other sinners. Few of us are malicious in our intent, yet we say or do things that cause pain to others. When we hurt each other, our goal is to get back to showing love for one another as quickly as possible.

Love and Conflict and Love Again

Sin initiates a potential conflict between two people, but a sinful reaction brings an argument to full fruition and perpetuates it. The truth is that we don't have to react to sin with sin. 1 Peter 4:8 teaches how to best prevent and end an argument: "Above all, love each other deeply, because love covers over a multitude of sins." When we love the way Jesus loves us, it helps us to "overlook an insult" (Proverbs 12:16). It also helps those we work with to give us grace when we sin against them or they misunderstand us.

1 Corinthians 8:1 says, "Knowledge puffs up while love builds up." Just because we see things a certain way or think we are right doesn't mean we love. Just because we are right doesn't mean we are righteous. In fact, when we win an argument, we lose the battle for unity with one another. In 2006 I helped plant the campus ministry in Ashland, Oregon. When I first arrived, I didn't have transportation of my own. I borrowed the minister's bike to get around town, and on my first ride it broke down. I gave it back to him and told him what had happened but didn't offer to help fix it. Later that summer I borrowed a sister's car. And as soon as I pushed in the clutch, the clutch cable snapped—and just before she needed to head back to Seattle. Again, I didn't offer to help pay to get it fixed.

Neither situation was my fault. I was right in the fact that they weren't my fault, but I wasn't righteous in the way I treated my brother and sister. The minister explained how he would never have asked me to pay to fix the bike, but it would have been a gesture that made him feel good about me borrowing things from him. I was forever changed.

Our relationships with one another are far more important than our being right or God's money that he has made us stewards of. In fact, Jesus calls us to lend to our enemies "without expecting to get anything back" (Luke 6:35). On the other hand, we are also supposed to "let no debt remain outstanding, except the continuing debt to love one another, for whoever loves others has fulfilled the law" (Romans 13:8). In short, if there is going to be an argument between disciples, it should be over who can serve the other, not who can receive. We are told that money, things of this world, shouldn't ever stand between us because our relationships and love are way more important!

Proverbs 27:6 says, "Wounds from a friend can be trusted, but an enemy multiplies kisses." When people know that we truly care about them, they are willing to hear the corrections and rebukes. Most of us fall into one of two categories: we put so much on the gentle side of love that we don't have the difficult conversations that help call people to obey Jesus; or we are so focused on making everyone perfect that people feel beaten down by the relentless standards. Instead, a healthy balance of gentle and tough love is what helps people to change long term.

In John 15:15 Jesus says he has started calling the disciples friends instead of servants. Jesus walked with the disciples every day, all day. We obviously can't do the same, but we can talk to each other and be friends with each other. Personally, I believe that technology is a double-edged sword, powerful and dangerous at the same time. However, when used the right way it can be a tool for building real relationships.

DO NOT MISHEAR ME! I am not talking about the superficial relationships created on social media and over text. We can't always be face to face, but we can pick up the phone and talk to one another. On the other hand, sitting and talking about nothing is too often substituted for being real and vulnerable. Jesus was especially vulnerable with the apostles at the Garden of Gethsemane just before his crucifixion. My wife has that same gut-check-level honesty with the women she works with. This helps them to be comfortable and able to talk to her about anything. When people know you aren't perfect, they will open up and be real in return, but no one likes talking to a robot.

A big part of Jesus' example was simply living life with his disciples, eating together and going about their day together. Spend time living life together with other people. One disciple I worked with years ago told me that his favorite time together was going to the hardware store with me one day. From then on, every other time we got together I taught him how to weld as we built a smoker for my father-in-law. While we built, we talked about how he was doing and about God. He later told me that those were some of the best discipling moments.

Matthew 17:1 shows us that Jesus took a few of his closest friends on a spiritual outing. He was preaching, teaching, healing, and sharing the gospel with his disciples. Are we spiritually active in our times with one another? I love this story of Jesus taking his closest three to the mountain together. When I'm not close to someone I work with, I take them out backpacking with me. One of my best friends was on staff in San Antonio with me; however, we had a rocky start. I had never spent a lot of time getting to know him, so we were cordial but not close. So I planned an overnight backpacking trip to a place called Lost Maples. We hiked, talked, swam, enjoyed the colorful maple trees, and got deep with one another. That time of bonding out in the wilderness was the turning point in our friendship, and we quickly became best friends right afterward.

Pray for Each Other

Jesus was a man of prayer. He did it all the time!

In John 17 Jesus prays for the disciples. How would you feel if you stepped into a discipling time knowing that the person had been praying for you? I recently restored a brother whose mother had been a part of a small prayer group with my wife. When we got together for the first time, I asked him: "Did you know that there's a group of women who have been praying for you consistently for the past few months?" His mind was blown to see how God had been working in his life through prayer. He was also extremely grateful for that group of women!

Prayer is powerful! Through prayer God has frequently revealed to me how to approach and handle a situation I was clueless about. Prayer heals like nothing I have ever seen before. Whenever two disciples have a conflict with each other, my first piece of advice is for them to pray for each other every day. It's a difficult pill to swallow, but it melts our hearts for one another. Prayer takes our own selfishness out of the way and helps us to focus on the other, just as Philippians 2 teaches us.

Jesus prayed by himself, and he prayed with his disciples. When we are together and united in prayer it invokes the presence of God. Historically and today, prayer gets God moving in our lives. It's like a thirsty car that finally gets the gas it needs. If you read through the book of Acts, they were constantly praying together, and the Spirit acted! When they didn't know what to do after Jesus had left, they went back and prayed together (Acts 1). Shortly after, one of the most amazing events in the Scriptures happened during Pentecost. Prayer together heals friendships and broken marriages. We don't pray together enough. What better way to help someone follow Jesus than to get on our knees and be in the presence of God together?

Keep Listening

People want to be heard! James 1:19 says, "Everyone should be quick to listen, slow to speak and slow to become angry." Why be slow to speak? Because you can always say more, but you can't easily undo saying too much or being too harsh.

God calls us to be quick to listen, so be present and stay focused! Nothing is more discouraging than someone who gives you the repeated "uh huh" response while focusing on their phone or something else seemingly more important than you. That communicates that we aren't listening and that we don't really care. It says that what I'm doing or thinking is more important than you. Interrupting is another anti-listening device. It's usually born from a lack of patience on our part. For me it's easy to see the issue and find a solution to something before someone finishes their story.

However, I've also been on the other side of the table when I've been interrupted before being able to finish communicating important details. There is a time and place for it, for example, when someone is being rude or negatively demonstrative, but interrupting should be an exception instead of the norm. Lately I've had to work on shutting down people's ideas too quickly. I can very rapidly analyze a situation and see its pitfalls or chances for success. When it's not a good idea, I list the reasons why the idea won't work, which just winds up making people feel like I didn't listen or that I don't care for their input. That's not the case, and a simple "Let me think about that" almost always helps them to feel better even if the resulting answer is still "no."

One of the scariest things for people is to communicate to their discipler how the discipler has hurt them. A huge part of listening is being humble. Whenever someone brings up issues they have with me—and they do, because I'm a sinner—I always fight to find something I can own up to. If they have the guts to talk to us, then we need to have the humility to listen. A part of that means racing to apologize for what we've done. *Even when they are wrong,* "be slow to become angry."

When I see things that they have mis-said or gotten wrong, I usually wait for a follow-up conversation to bring those things up. Otherwise, the discussion quickly turns into a mud-slinging event. If you lead the way with humility for an entire conversation, it will normally bring a humble response when following up.

Ask and Listen to Understand

Proverbs 20:5 says, "The purposes of a person's heart are deep waters, but one who has insight draws them out." This scripture has led me to great success when I have put it into practice, and I have suffered great pitfalls when I haven't. I love to figure things out. I enjoy trying to figure out how a movie is going to end before it's finished. I like to try and understand how a building or machine was built. And I love jumping into situations and trying to understand what's going on between people. It's something I enjoy, and something those around me say I'm pretty good at. With all of that, though, I still frequently find myself jumping into a situation and being wrong about my initial understanding of it. Why? Because when we are dealing with people, the truth of a matter is frequently buried, and we have to draw it out.

If there is conflict between you and another, seek to understand, not to be understood. When both parties only want to be heard, resolution can never come.

Ask questions. Jesus had the amazing ability to know a person's heart without even having to talk to them (Mark 2:8). He knew what the Pharisees were thinking. We don't have that gift; however, we can ask questions. Questions draw out the heart, and it's something that Jesus frequently did when being cornered by the Pharisees. Questions bring humility to both parties and a quick resolution. But "to answer before listening—that is folly and shame" (Proverbs 18:13).

Clear and Careful Communication

There are many nuances in language. What we say can be a spark that sets a forest on fire (James 3:5–6). Our tone, pitch, word choice, facial reactions, and body language all do a majority of the talking for us. A few years ago I was sincerely trying to compliment another disciple during a conversation. However, they thought I was being sarcastic, and an entire family was cross with me until we were able to talk and I could clear things up. Asking the simple question, "What did you mean?" could have saved a lot of hurt feelings. Many times we are oblivious to what we are communicating outside of the language we are using.

In high school, my gymnastics coach asked me to go to the other side of the gym and work on a move called a Yurchenko Full. Basically, it's a roundoff on the vault with a straight-bodied backward flip and a full twist, all before sticking the landing. In response, I cocked my head to one side, squinted with my left eye and raised my right eyebrow. He proceeded to reprimand me for being prideful and told me to just do what he asked. I was simply visualizing how to do the move in my head but quickly realized that my thinking face comes across as angry and defiant!

What we say and how we say it matters! When we counsel marrieds, we find that most of their arguments are started and prolonged by miscommunicating and misunderstanding. Ten-minute discussions turn into three-hour arguments because we micro-analyze each other's words and highlight what is wrong. We need to be careful and think about what the person we are talking to is hearing, not just what we are saying. 2 Timothy 2:14 (ESV) teaches us "not to quarrel about words, which does no good, but only ruins the hearers." How many times do we get nit-picky about the words someone else is using? It's pointless! God said it best: "Do not let any unwholesome talk come out of your mouths, but only what is helpful for building others up according to their needs, that it may benefit those who listen" (Ephesians 4:29).

Matthew 22:37–40 says, "You shall love the Lord your God and with all your heart and with all your soul and with all your mind. This is the great and first commandment. And a second is like it: You shall love your neighbor as yourself. On these two commandments depend all the Law and the Prophets." All the scriptures we've looked at so far hinge on loving God and others. They depend on loving others as do the Law and the Prophets. I wholeheartedly believe that the context of the entire Bible is love. A discipling relationship with this same context will soar to new heights and glorify God!

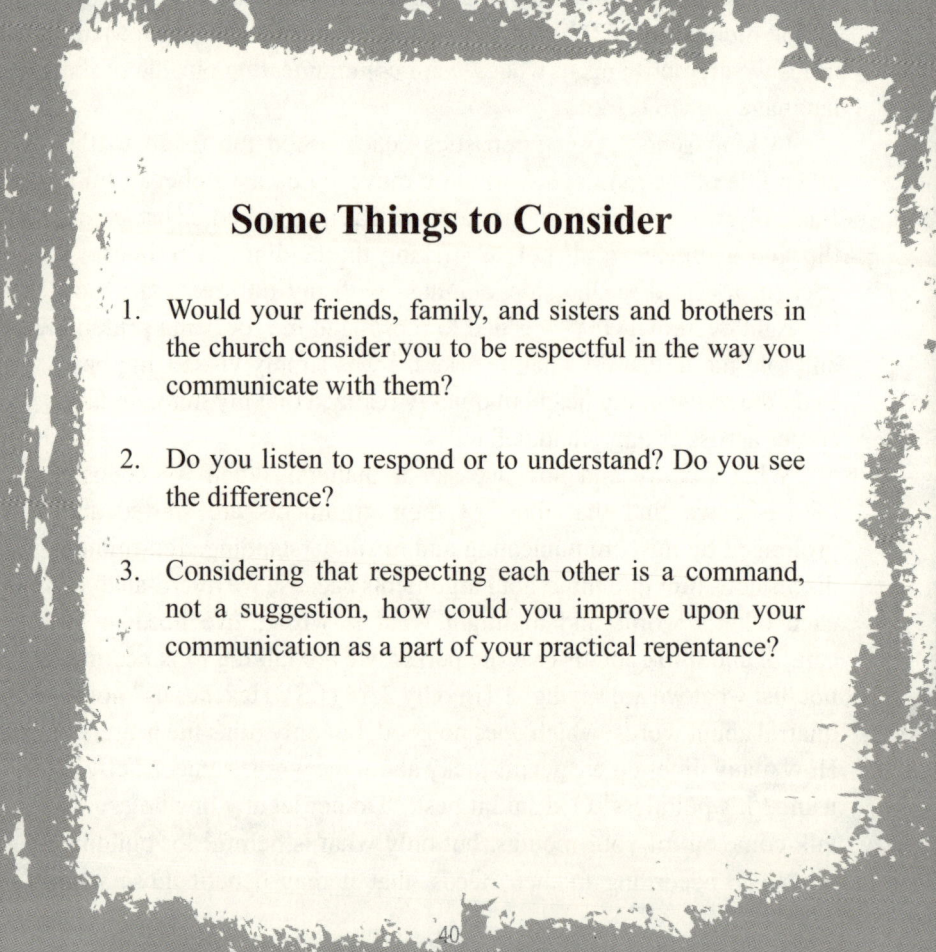

Some Things to Consider

1. Would your friends, family, and sisters and brothers in the church consider you to be respectful in the way you communicate with them?

2. Do you listen to respond or to understand? Do you see the difference?

3. Considering that respecting each other is a command, not a suggestion, how could you improve upon your communication as a part of your practical repentance?

5

A Relationship Founded in Love

Therefore, as God's chosen people, holy and dearly loved, clothe yourselves with compassion, kindness, humility, gentleness and patience. Bear with each other and forgive one another if any of you has a grievance against someone. Forgive as the Lord forgave you. And over all these virtues put on love, which binds them all together in perfect unity.
—Colossians 3:12–14

Love is the umbrella under which the Lord has placed all our one-another directives in this life. In this book's appendix we give a model to visualize this point of view. We hope through this first section of the book, as we redefine these one-another commands, themes such as patience, kindness, humility, and listening will become more of a deep conviction. Actually, these are not new at all, but it seems nowadays we don't start here. These are firm foundations in our one-another relationships in Christ. Without them, it is very difficult for us to learn to trust and protect one another. Without them, we may never learn to overcome sin together. Without them, intentional discipling maybe exist only in our imaginations.

Another one of my best friends and a brother, Omar Clark, will guide us through some considerations about how love, even though a huge topic, is the only way in which we can build true relationships that can sustain a unified discipling culture within the body.

Coauthor Introduction:Omar Clark

Omar Clark is part of the New York Church of Christ (Queens ministry) and has been a disciple for over twenty years. He has served in the Port Elizabeth, South Africa church as a part of the "One-Year Challenge" that turned into three years. It was a great time of spiritual learning and inspiration for Omar. He's excited to share some perspectives of love in discipling relationships.

Love: Redefined

Love. This is such a heavy word, equally as weighty as the question, "What's the meaning of life?" Everyone wants love, seeks love, needs love. Jesus even says that wicked people arc capable of love! (Matthew 5:46–47). With so much emphasis on love and our natural inclination to seek loving environments and relationships, how do we love in a way that not only drives us closer together, but also closer to God?

To answer this question, I think it's important to talk about the opposite of love (sometimes, things are best described by what they are not). This is easy enough, right? The opposite of love is…fear! But is it really that simple? I'll direct us to one of my favorite movies to further the discussion: *A Bronx Tale*. Who doesn't love a good Robert De Niro flick? If you haven't seen the film yet, you're either too young or too late. A key scene breaks down Sonny's (gangster and street mentor of our young protagonist) view on his preferred environment when Calogero (our protagonist) asks a critical question: "Is it better to be loved, or feared?"

Sonny, unsurprisingly, chooses fear. How else is a gangster in charge of old mob territory in the Bronx supposed to maintain control? And that's exactly what this way of understanding is designed to do… maintain control. This type of fear-based environment may produce desired behavior, but it will also foster resentment.

This discussion on fear is important because we need to understand (and even accept) how we can sometimes allow our worldly constructs of fear to be a means to an end. However, 1 John says that perfect love drives out fear. We need to evaluate our use of fear as a means, and whether we are getting to a genuine end. Ultimately, God desires obedience motivated by our love for him, which comes from a deep understanding of his love for us. That's God's standard, his requirement. It's all he asks and all he's ever wanted. The question for us is:

Are we demanding something different from one another than what God demands?

Do we want something that appears to be genuine obedience so long as our attendance is up, or our conversions are at pace? Would we choose this at risk of forgoing a genuine relationship with God? If we understand God this way, how do we understand one another?

You may protest my take on fear because in the back (or front) of your mind, you're recalling scriptures about "the fear of the Lord" being "the beginning of wisdom." You would be correct to approach with scrutiny and caution a discussion on fear that paints fear negatively. I'll do you a favor and reword things slightly so we can all digest the topic a little more easily. How about I submit my own amplified version of 1 John like this: "Perfect righteous love drives out unrighteous fear"? Aha! So there is a place for fear! Yes, there sure is. Nevertheless, this part of the chapter will focus on love-based environments.

To Rebuke or Not to Rebuke

Rebuke. It's one of the very first things we're taught about as disciples of Jesus. If "The Word" is someone's first sitting Bible study in our fellowship, they will learn that a rebuke (2 Timothy 3:16) is "a harsh correction" reserved for when a person sins in some way that they were previously corrected for. In other words, they should have known better by now.

In our church culture, we have embraced these "harsh corrections" as character-building words or acts of love. Very rarely a region hasn't heard a leader preach about the good ol' days full of healthy rebukes. It's like this romantic pastime that an older generation feels the newer generation is missing out on. Tied to this idea was the flawed acceptance of the NIV1977 and 1984 rendering of Matthew 11:12, which reads: "From the days of John the Baptist until now, the kingdom of heaven has been forcefully advancing, and forceful men lay hold of it." The call for us as a brotherhood was to embrace a forceful, heavy-handed culture, and frequent rebukes were an essential part of it.

There are reasons why this forceful element was embraced and why it is flawed. I think one overlapping reason is human nature. The opening monologue in the first volume of *The Lord of the Rings* says, "Nine rings were given to the race of men, who, above all else, desire power." Whether intentionally or not, we can embrace flawed renderings of Scripture when they give us license to feel powerful and accomplish our goals (or make our sermon points). Is this what the scriptures in 2 Timothy 3 and Matthew 11 are meant to convey? Questioning this deserves our attention and requires careful inspection. This is not intended to be an academic examination of these texts, but a brief overview may prove worthwhile here.

When I really want to study out the original meaning of a passage as best I can without being anywhere near a Greek or Hebrew scholar, I typically do two things. The first is I look at several translations of the scripture to see what the prevailing renderings are. The second is I look up the word in a concordance and use (are you ready for my deep scholarship?) Thayer's Lexicon to try to understand its original meaning. I might consult some biblical commentary, but not necessarily and not often. My tool of choice for the longest has been blueletterbible.org (that's a freebie).

So what did I find when I finally examined this text?

Fourteen out of fifteen translations (using the list from Blue Letter Bible) render Matthew 11:12 as "the kingdom of heaven has suffered violence" (ESV) or some variant thereof. They all (save the NLT) view people *outside* of the kingdom as being forceful and aggressive. How did John the Baptist experience this violence? Well, he was jailed and beheaded. The culture of disciples of Jesus being forceful or aggressive toward the world or toward each other is based on one or two translations that render it that way. Even the NIV doesn't translate it as "forcefully advancing" anymore.

The point is, while our fellowship has served as a refuge for lost souls and restored many a broken spirit to the Creator, Satan has also insidiously worked to instill a sense of fear in our relationships. If we're going to be free to love one another as the Scriptures call us to, we have to sift this forceful nature out of our mentalities. Our "one anothering" will be influenced by the culture that surrounds it.

Is there a place for healthy rebuke (e.g., Nathan rebukes David)? To study 2 Timothy 3, I decided to examine a few choice examples of rebuking in God's kingdom as it occurs in the New Testament. Yes, these are choice (implication "my choice") examples, but this isn't an exhaustive discussion on the topic either. To draw your own conclusion, you'll have to really be a Berean and study the Scriptures to see if what I'm saying is true.

Case 1: Get Behind Me, Satan!

Imagine the most disheartening conversation you've had with anyone in the last five years (sorry to bring up old stuff). Now after bringing that back along with all the possible visceral responses, compare that to a live conversation with God, where God in the flesh (and audibly to your face), calls you Satan. Now that is a rough day. What a discouraging conversation! Why would Jesus use such harsh language? Without getting into a full dissertation, Peter in this passage is elevating himself to the point of telling God what to do. Essentially, he wants to alter God's plan because he thinks he is wiser.

We do this all the time, don't we? But this instance is a little different. If Peter had his way, Jesus would not have gone to the cross! And where would that leave all of humanity? God's children would be without hope, and there would only be a looming destruction for us all. Peter's will goes completely against God's game plan. His position is very worthy of rebuke!

Case 2: Woe to You, Pharisees!

Our review of Jesus rebuking Peter will seem tame when we look at Matthew 23. Jesus unleashes a verbal lashing fit for the heard-hearted religious authorities of the day. In every way possible, Jesus makes known to them and to their hearers that they are hypocrites and should be "followed" with extreme scrutiny. Why did he give such a rebuke here? Well, let's look at what was at stake according to Jesus:

> *"But woe to you, scribes and Pharisees, hypocrites! You lock up the kingdom of heaven from people. For you don't go in, and you don't allow those entering to go in"* (Matthew 23:13 HCSB).

45

Jesus views their attitudes and behaviors as stumbling blocks to innocent people. His yeast metaphor is apt for how they operate (see verse 15). Jesus' rebuke here speaks to a culture of pride, disenfranchisement, and spiritual poverty. As Jesus points out, these personalities occupied the seat of Moses, so they still held some religious authority. The potential to lead swaths of people away from God was too huge. It's unimaginable to think how many souls would have been led astray over the centuries if this rebuke were not recorded.

What's common between these two cases is that Jesus confronts ideas that, if carried out or allowed to continue without being addressed, would completely derail God's plan of redemption for humanity. These are extreme situations, and I argue that our rebukes today should also be reserved for the extreme. Not the rudimentary everyday Christianity that requires regular correction, but for the outlandish ideas or extreme behavior that would prevent people from being able to get in contact with the blood of Jesus. Still think a rebuke is a "harsh correction" that demands regular use in one's Christian walk?

I'd like to briefly examine one more case: that of David and Nathan. We know the story from 2 Samuel 11. David is home during a war with the Philistines, sees Bathsheba, summons her into his court, sleeps with her, impregnates her, attempts a coverup, and finally, has one of his most devoted soldiers murdered to wipe the slate clean. A mulligan. We won't go over it in detail here, but you should read it on your own for context. There are a few key points I'd like to discuss.

1. This action required the knowledge of all his servants to be carried out. No, I'm not highlighting their guilt or role as accomplices, however valid that may be.

2. After it was carried out, several months passed by as Bathsheba's pregnancy progressed (it took nine months to birth a baby even back then, right?).

3. We only know of one man who honestly confronted David about it all: Nathan the prophet.

We can talk about how wicked David might have been, or how cowardly his servants might have been, or even how slow Nathan might have been to arrive on the scene. What I'd like to question is this: What type of environment had David created in which none of his servants would question his decision-making or interject a warning when they saw blatant sin happening before them and God? Was David somehow known as a harsh leader during this time? A king with unquestionable authority?

What is more unquestionable as I've studied this passage over the years is this: David has a boundary. While he was widely loved and admired as a man after God's own heart, there was a piece of himself that others around him clearly felt was inaccessible at the time of this tragedy. David, once the persecuted, becomes the coveter and persecutor, and no one is willing to redirect him. The guard dogs were patrolling the perimeter, snipers were at the towers watching out into the fields, and the drawbridge was closed. Whether or not David intended to steal Bathsheba the entire time on his way home from the battlefield is irrelevant. What matters now is the inaccessibility his community had to his heart.

Have you ever been afraid of approaching someone in the fellowship because of a realistic expectation of an adverse reaction to hearing the truth about themselves, regardless of how gentle your approach? Resistance, dismissal, defensiveness, anger, denial, spite, belittling, reverse psychological judgment. Have you experienced any of that when attempting to lovingly tell someone that in the midst of their sin they're somehow missing Jesus? Was that person ever you?

I wonder what the king's men were fearing? A harsh dismissal? Suspension without pay? Losing their livelihood? Losing their life? Hey, if it happened to Uriah…

As "rulers" of our own kingdoms, what sort of environment do we create for our brothers and sisters around us? I think this is directly applicable to anyone in a leadership position, but equally applicable to our personal relationships.

The Impact of Culture

I've been blessed. Of course, so has everyone who has stumbled upon this remarkable truth called the kingdom of God. What I mean is, I've been blessed even beyond finding this incredible, loving environment. You see, my journey in God's kingdom has taken me all over the United States, into different fellowships, into the Caribbean, and into Africa. No, I'm not rich and no, I'm not blessed just because I've been able to travel. What makes me feel blessed is that I've been exposed to how the kingdom of God is manifested among different cultures. I've been able to compare godly fellowships as they've been (for better or worse) infused with the culture around them. I've come to realize that as far as people groups go, the kingdom of heaven feels most natural to me when expressed through Eastern cultures. Maybe this is because our entire spiritual history is Eastern.

My time in Port Elizabeth, South Africa was like no other in my walk. It may be partly due to small-church culture (the congregation hovers around fifty members), but I think in a broader sense, the communal culture of South Africa helped to infuse the church with palpable familial ties. I never felt like I owned more homes than when I lived there. I picked up and dropped off people's children at school. I held keys and occupied homes more often than I can recount, whether or not the owners were home or even in town. I've cooked more meals, driven more cars, carried more babies, slept on more couches, and interacted with more relatives of my church sisters and brothers than I can ever remember doing with such frequency and nearly blind trust. Could Jesus' promise in Matthew 19 of receiving 100 times more homes, brothers, sisters, fathers, mothers, children, and fields be more literal than I've taken it to be? **My experience says, "Yes!"**

In comparison, although my time in the United States has been transformative since becoming a disciple, I can clearly feel the difference between Eastern and Western culture as expressed through our fellowships. We love, but in a way that is a bit tempered by our tendency as a nation toward individualism. Love in the churches here is certainly leaps and bounds above the world's love, but there's something missing that maybe only experience can clarify.

It may be time to stop exporting our Westernized ideas for fellowship as best practices and begin importing ideas from our sisters and brothers across the great pond.

All about Perspective
Matthew 28:18–20. We all know it. Not just in our fellowship; the Christian religious world knows it. "Make disciples of all nations, baptizing them in the name of the Father and of the Son and of the

Holy Spirit, and teaching them to obey everything I have commanded you. And surely I am with you always, to the very end of the age."

There's a charge and a promise in there. There are also implications. The implication for relationships is that we are in dire need of one another. How can we teach the nations if we have no one who can teach? We already know Jesus' multidisciplinary style of teaching (didactic, relational, example-setting, etc.). We need one another to continue teaching and learning his commands. If we do this, he will be with us! Our relationships with each other have a direct effect on whether God is with us.

That's one way to view this passage. In truth, I don't have much to gripe about with that explanation, except for one thing. Why did I present you with this view on the passage? Well, because I've heard it preached that way. Now I want to offer a slightly alternative view with the following implications.

We are in dire need of relationships—relationships that help to refine us into the image of Christ so that we are prepared for his return. His design was for us to be deeply committed to relationship with each other, as in his prayer in John 17 ("that all of them may be one"). Jesus leaves his disciples with an incredible task before them. Essentially, they were meant to pass on this message of salvation, fight against Satan's plan to destroy God's church, and save as many souls as possible in the process. All the while, they were to love one another they way Jesus taught them to love.

How in the world would they accomplish such a huge task? I'm reminded of *The Matrix* when Neo has a private session with Cypher. Cypher poses the question, "Did he tell you why he did it? Why you're here?" Neo responds affirmatively. Cypher's next sentiments are priceless: "What a mind job! So you're here to save the world. What do you say to something like that?"

That's exactly the task before the disciples. How could they possibly carry this out? Now we get to Jesus' promise: "And surely I am with you always, to the very end of the age."

The promise of fellowship between Jesus and his disciples isn't just about those who were hearing him at that moment. This promise is to the church. It's God himself who promises a kingdom that the gates of Hades will never overcome. The church a part of that kingdom. That's why this promise is to the "end of the age." As such, this isn't a conditional promise of togetherness. It is an unconditional pledge of love and support as God's dearly loved child goes into the world to proclaim him.

So what's the big deal? Won't both perspectives result in the same behavior or bring about the same results? Possibly, if we're measuring performance. But if we're measuring intimacy and confidence in God's love, quite possibly not. Let's analyze the motivations:

1) The IF-THEN schema: If I make disciples, baptize, and continue teaching, then God will be with me. Corollary: If I do not make disciples, baptize, and continue teaching, then God will not be with me. This view emphasizes a reward/punishment schema. It may drive you to share your faith, study the Bible with people, and have discipling times (whether you want to or not!), but at the risk of great insecurity over God's closeness to you when you don't do these things. This is the view that we can take when we look at Jesus as primarily speaking to us individually in Matthew 28.

a. Human relationship translation: If this is how we view our walk with God, it can look like great insecurity in our human interactions. If we forget to call or meet up with said brother or sister, do we think they will pull away from us?

2) The AND schema: I'll take up the charge to make disciples, baptize, and continue teaching. As I stumble along the way, God will always be with me. This view emphasizes God's unconditional love. Truly understanding this will result in many of the same behaviors (sharing your faith, studying the Bible with people, having discipling times), but without the risk of feeling insecure that God has somehow left you when you aren't "performing well." This is the view we can thrive in when we look at Jesus as primarily speaking to his church, his bride whom he will never forsake and who he promised would never be overcome by the gates of Hades.

a. Human relationship translation: If this is how we view our walk with God, it can look like very healthy human interactions. If you forget to call, forget a birthday, or are somehow selfish in another way, you are sure that the love we extend and receive remains intact.

Sure, there are some legitimate "if-then's" in Scripture, but once we enter a relationship with God (i.e., we are the bride he will never forsake), Scripture far more describes his interaction with us in "and" terminology. Embracing a secure agape love relationship with God will help to ensure love for one another while we're on earth.

This can be difficult. I myself struggle with wanting to relegate some of my brotherly relationships to an if-then schema. When I can't take someone else's imperfection anymore, or when someone's sin seems unchanging, things get real! What helps me to stay grounded is how I feel on the other end. I know when I hurt someone, whether intentionally or not, there's just one thing I desire most. That is to feel truly forgiven in their presence. Let's talk about forgiveness next.

Some Things to Consider

1. Would your friends, family, and brothers and sisters in the church consider you to be more loving or more forceful if given those two options? Which way would they lean?

2. How do you view situations when or where a rebuke is needed? Likewise, when or where it is not needed?

3. Considering the Great Commission from Jesus (Matthew 28), what commands should we be focused on teaching others?

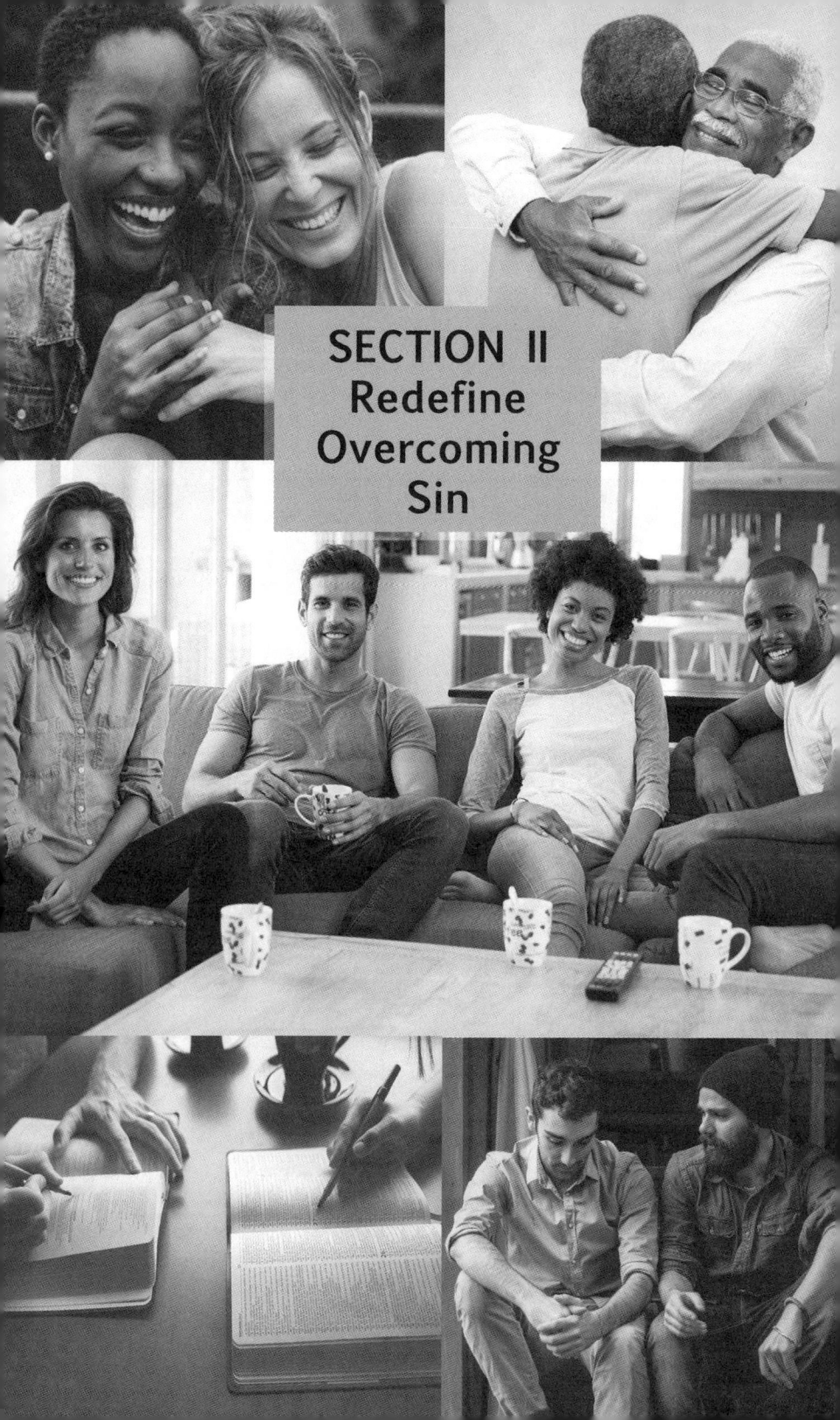

SECTION II
Redefine Overcoming Sin

6

A Relationship with Vulnerability

Brothers and sisters, if someone is caught in a sin, you who live by the Spirit should restore that person gently. But watch yourselves, or you also may be tempted. Carry each other's burdens, and in this way you will fulfill the law of Christ.

—Galatians 6:1–2

In the first section of the book, we covered in depth how to treat one another with love and humility. I really believe if we get that on straight with some newfound conviction, this second section will be quite organic. An organic fruit of love could be greater trust and security among one another, which leads to a safe culture that breeds open dialogue about sin, mistakes, and failures—hopefully a culture where we all help to "carry" and support one another, which is clearly God's will.

I studied the Bible with this next brother, whom I love deeply. His name is Alex Jackson, and I feel he is someone I totally trust. We can talk about it all… We really do! Let's take a good look at his perspectives on the significance of having vulnerability in all our Chirstian relationships.

_____ **Coauthor Introduction: Alex Jackson** _____

 Alex Jackson was born, bred, schooled, and converted all within a five-mile radius in the heart of Atlanta, Georgia. He became a Christian in campus ministry in 2006 at Georgia Tech and is grateful for the skills built through friendship and Bible studies. One area that Alex feels comes up regardless of race, religion, or creed is that vulnerability is hard—yet so attractive. As he looks around at today's society, Alex sees it as one of the few unifying concepts in an ever-dividing world. He now lives in Marietta, Georgia with his wife, Jasmine, and son, Lev Judah.

Vulnerability: Redefined

I would like to redefine vulnerability for disciples as not being the ability to share fears and sin, but the ability to courageously face life and seek to be more like Jesus.

If you did a word search of "vulnerability" in the Bible, you would come up lacking. And you would think a word like openness, which is often used in Christian fellowships, would be more common, but no.

Yet the concept at the heart of these words is fundamental to spreading the Christian faith. In this chapter, we seek to redefine vulnerability and its essential role in having deep relationships.

What Hinders Vulnerability

In conversation with my sisters and brothers I asked for their insight about what hinders vulnerability, and the overwhelming response was: **a lack of trust.**

Everything tells us that we can't trust (fill in the blank) so we choose not to open up to that person. While this may not be a problem for the average human, it creates a stumbling block for disciples of Jesus, who are called to love their neighbor (Matthew 22:39). How do I love a neighbor I don't trust? How can I build a relationship with a neighbor I'm not willing to open up to?

I'm starting to believe searching for such an answer may solve a lot of the church's "PR" problems. Statements are strengthened that "the church" is judgmental or bigoted when doctrine is thrown about more than opportunities for trust and love. Without extending opportunities for vulnerability and building trust, we run the risk of living an isolated and meaningless life.

Vulnerability, Openness: What Does It All Mean?

Let's explore some terms. You may be asking what I mean by vulnerability. The dictionary defines it as the quality or state of being exposed to the possibility of being attacked or harmed, either physically or emotionally. "Openness" is noted as a synonym, and in this chapter "openness" and "vulnerability" will be used interchangeably. Both words are popular in our current culture, along with terms like emotional intelligence and sensitivity, to define a need in our world for connection and relatability. Both words express ways to bring people together.

If you are familiar with Dr. Brené Brown, you know that vulnerability is her bread and butter. Dr. Brown is a popular Houston-based researcher who champions vulnerability and exposes its counterpoint, shame. In her book, *Daring Greatly,* I love her ability to redefine our stereotypes of vulnerability as weakness, defining it instead as "uncertainty, risk and emotional exposure."

Around the world, thought leaders like Jocko Willink and Justin Baldoni are also putting their own spin on a need to be honest, explore masculinity, and expose themselves to the possibility of attack. Regardless of the word used, the crux of the issue is found throughout the Scriptures because it is a quality of God.

Vulnerability and God

Let's look at the most widely publicized scripture in the world, John 3:16–17:

> For God so **loved** the world that he gave his one and only Son, that whoever believes in him shall not perish but have eternal life. For God did not send his Son into the world to condemn the world, but to save

the world through him (emphasis added).

This passage has at its core an opportunity to love, and you cannot love without vulnerability or emotional exposure. Love happens at the risk of rejection. But "God is love" (1 John 4:16), so he does expose himself to the risk of our rejection consistently and often. You can even see it as you continue in this passage, in John 3:19–21:

> *This is the verdict: Light has come into the world, but people loved darkness instead of light because their deeds were evil. Everyone who does evil hates the light, and will not come into the light for fear that their deeds will be exposed. But whoever lives by the truth comes into the light, so that it may be seen plainly that what they have done has been done in the sight of God.*

Here we see God showing his intention to love us as a son or daughter and our response of loving our darkness more than God. Meditation on this dichotomy has to lead me to question who I want to identify with more: God or my darkness?

Vulnerability and Discipling

You may be thinking, This is all well and great, but what does it have to do with discipling and redefinition? Well, **vulnerability at its core is an identity issue.**

If you identify as a disciple of Jesus and you seek to be like him, then you know there is a daily aspect of reflection that cannot be done without emotional exposure. If you are not a disciple of Jesus but you are engaging the concept of following him, you know how liberating and inspiring it is to see ordinary men and women speak with courage, knowing their confidence does not come from their accomplishments but from knowing Christ (Acts 4:13; Philippians 3:7–10).

I know God built vulnerability and openness into the fabric of how we relate to each other for a reason. It is only with a clear understanding of who we are in relation to God and one another that we can move forward together. Consistent emotional exposure is what keeps us in meaningful relationships. Without it we run the risk of living a life without trust and true connection.

Some Things to Consider

1. Would your friends, family, and brothers and sisters in the church consider you to be vulnerable?

2. Do you trust those around you?

3. What things from your past (or present) make trust hard?

4. Considering that trust is a command, not a suggestion, how could you improve upon trusting others as a part of your practical repentance?

7

A Relationship with Frequent Forgiveness

Be kind and compassionate to one another, forgiving each other, just as in Christ God forgave you.

—Ephesians 4:32

Enough said. Hard to live out, but we are called to the kind of forgiveness this scripture describes.

As we call Omar Clark back to the stage, he will share just how critical a role forgiveness plays in everything we do in our discipling relationships. It is foundational for us in overcoming sin together. Just think, without this mercy from God, our sin remains. And so does the fair penalty.

Forgiveness: Redefined

I've dated a few times in my journey as a disciple. One legitimate question people ask about my dating experience is: "What lessons have you learned?" I'll share three key ones with you: communication, communication, communication. Boy, does it ever take work and patience to get communication right. But once you get it, it can make that ship sail much more smoothly. So practice communication.

This question, however, remains: what happens when communication simply fails? At that point, I hope you have been growing in your ability to forgive! This is not a dating advice book, but I use this example to emphasize just how practically and critically forgiveness is in all relationships.

Think of communication like a technical skill that you acquire. Maybe it's your ability to shoot a jump shot as accurately as say, Steph Curry (or BJ Armstrong for you older heads). It's an amazing spectacle watching players at the top of their game make shot after shot during a season. Still, there's one guarantee amid all the excitement of watching your favorite players smash 3-pointers from half court during the playoffs. Eventually, no matter how good the player is, they will miss.

That's communication. It gets better with practice, but the miss is bound to occur. So what happens when a player misses a shot? Well, the team's offensive rebound game better be on point. No rebounds, no second chances, no wins. That's forgiveness.

God's "I Can't"

So how's your forgiveness? At the end of the day, it's all that matters. Jesus doesn't mince words with this! In the parable of the unforgiving servant, he sums it up with, "This is how my heavenly Father will treat each of you unless you forgive your brother or sister from your heart" (Matthew 18:35). **God will not forgive unforgiveness.**

Everyone has their breaking point. In our modern vernacular, we loosely use the phrase "I can't" to denote when we've reached our limit. Most of the time I hear this used, it's playful: "I can't with you!" Well, God's "I can't" isn't playful at all. It's a serious limit and one that we must understand if we are going to be his followers. You don't want to put learning to forgive on hold and get to judgment day only to hear God say, "I can't with you!"

Why Is Forgiveness So Important?

Forgiveness is definitely on the world's radar. It can be controversial when we look at reactions to radical Christian forgiveness, but otherwise forgiveness has taken on a new-age focus that centers on the self. Forgiveness (according to the world) is about letting people go, along with all their mess and distractions. It's about liberating yourself from needing to be "righted" with individuals or organizations who have wronged us. It's all about peace of mind and mental well-being.

Is that God's plan for forgiveness? God's purpose for forgiveness is opposite that of the world. While the world's forgiveness is about the person doing the forgiving, God's forgiveness is about the person being forgiven. Sure, there is some liberation that comes with forgiveness, but that's a byproduct. It's not the focus with God. In other words, forgiveness is an act that allows for reconciliation. When the world forgives, it's "I forgive you, now goodbye!" When God forgives, it's "I forgive you, now come closer."

This is what our entire salvation is based upon. God didn't send Jesus to die on the cross just so he could send us away with a clear conscience and be free from the stress that we've undoubtedly caused him. God sent Jesus to die so that we could grow in a relationship together and ultimately be together in relationship for eternity. Our entire walk with God is predicated on forgiveness! It should follow that forgiving one another should be modeled on the forgiving nature of God.

What Forgiveness Does

When Jesus came to die and offer us forgiveness, technically it washed away our sins. I want to be sensitive because that's of paramount importance, but I think sometimes we can become robotic and forget the emotional side of things when we only focus on the technicality that was before us (our sin).

So, what did forgiveness do for humankind on an emotional level? Forgiveness frees us in our emotional capacity to sincerely approach God as the Father who extends love and accepts us in spite of our faults.

Let's look at two examples:

• **The Prodigal Son (Luke 15:11–32).** We know the story. The younger son requests his share of the inheritance and goes off to live a lavish (and foolish) life. He spends all his money and has to come back to his father's house. How embarrassing, right? As you read the text, let's examine it in light of Jesus' audience: tax collectors and sinners (the defiled), pharisees and scribes (the "clean"). Jesus likely makes this story up with Jewish characters. This young Jewish man completely dishonors his father. This is no small sin! Several places in the law deem such behavior as worthy of death (e.g., Deuteronomy 21:18–22).

Yet the father does something unique from the outset. He doesn't bring such rebellious behavior before the elders (could the father already have forgiveness in mind?). Had he done so, the village would have stoned him before he could say "Shalom."

Next, the boy squanders all his father's inheritance. That's like Esau forsaking his birthright! No respectable Jew would ever do this (see Naboth's response to Ahab in 1 Kings 21:1–3). Safeguarding his inheritance would honor his father and provide proof of his stake in the tribes of Israel. Asking for his inheritance ahead of time basically says, "You're dead to me, Dad!" Then he goes and squanders it, which basically says, "You're dead to me, Israel!"

It gets worse from there. After he squanders it, he takes a job feeding pigs. What's wrong with that, you say? He's still Jewish! That's like permanent defilement! I wouldn't be surprised if he was around some swine carcasses in the process. Just read all of Leviticus 11 (verse 7 highlights pigs) to understand the disgust that would be on the faces of the Pharisees and scribes at this time. Maybe Jesus was making gross faces as he told it (that thought makes me laugh).

Oh, now you wanna come to your senses, huh boy?! That's how I'd want to respond. But when the son finally comes to his senses, I can only imagine him having one predominant feeling: shame. Could he look his father in the eye? How often did he have to rehearse that tired speech? He knows it's culturally impossible to return now, but was there any room in his father's heart? What incredibly heavy shame.

We know his father's response. He runs, embraces, doesn't even allow his son to finish his entire speech (there's significance in that too), and hastily prepares a feast for him. His love, manifested through his forgiveness, erases the shame. Forgiveness is the antidote for shame. When we consider all that the father had to forgive, it's clear to see that God doesn't count how far we've gone. God is far more interested in how far we'll come. He's ready for us as soon as we're ready for him.

I mentioned that there's significance in the father cutting off his son's speech. The rest of the speech was "Make me like one of your hired servants." The son is willing to be the least in his father's house, but his father doesn't allow him to take on this identity. This word, "make," is used throughout the gospels, but one of the most significant places where we see it is in the first gospel (in chronological order), Mark. You guessed it. Jesus uses it when he calls his first disciples. "I will make you fish for people" (HCSB).

The Greek word, *poieō,* is the same in both passages. Could it be that just as Jesus wanted to give his first followers a new identity and purpose according to his Father's will, the son in the story wants to change his own identity and purpose in the opposite manner? Astonishingly, the father never allows him to utter this new identity. His father only wants him to identify as his son, now forgiven. How crazy is that?

One of the major implications here is that we need to practice forgiveness with each other like God forgives us. In our story, forgiveness is offered when the offender is ready to repent, not after the offended has had enough time to process and get over the offense. What if we had to wait for God to "come out of his feelings" for him to forgive us?

When we think about forgiveness, we need to ask ourselves, "Is my forgiveness predicated on how I feel or if I'm ready, or rather on when my offender is ready to truly be reconciled?" **This...is not... easy.**

I'm certainly not suggesting that in our current sinful states, we are capable of handling all personalities at all times. That's not realistic (we're not God). However, when it's time to forgive, we need to make sure that somewhere in there is the thought of reconciliation. It may take time, and in extreme cases maybe there are some changes that need to be made before people can interact peaceably again. Still, I believe the Scriptures teach that a lack of willingness to reconcile is shy of the forgiveness that God wants us to embrace.

Look over at Luke 17:1–10. I'm reading the Holman Christian Standard Bible, and there's a subtitle break between verses 4 and 5. Try removing or ignoring that break and reading it as one continuous text. Jesus teaches his disciples that people will sin against us, and we should be ready for when that happens. How should we be ready?

With a forgiving heart! (verse 3). Seven times a day we must forgive (remember God's "I can't"?). Reading right through any subtitling, his followers respond to this with "Increase our faith!" The subsequent teaching on faith and duty are both now tied to forgiveness. We need faith to do it (although not much, according to Jesus) and it is our absolute duty as his servants. Let's take a look at our second case.

• **Joseph (Genesis 37–50).** Take some time to read and review this account on your own, but let's recall some of the things Joseph had to forgive:

1. He may have had to forgive his father for singling him out all those years, causing his brothers to resent him.

2. He had to forgive his brothers for resenting him, trying to kill him, and then leaving him for dead.

3. He had to forgive his cousins, the Ishmaelites (sons of grand-uncle Ishmael), for trading him as a slave to Egypt.

4. He had to forgive Potiphar's wife for attempting to seduce him day after day (Genesis 39:10) and then lying about it.

5. He had to forgive Potiphar for not believing him and jailing him.

6. He might have needed to ask God for forgiveness for the resentment he felt for being jailed for two years.

7. He had to forgive the chief cupbearer for forgetting about him after his release from prison.

8. After seeing his brothers again in Egypt, it appears to me like he had to forgive them all over again!

Joseph had a lot to forgive, and he certainly struggled with it. This is one of the most emotionally evocative passages dealing with forgiveness. It took Joseph some time, but he was able to do it. What helped him? I think a key factor was his relationship with God. Joseph was close enough to God to fit his story into God's bigger picture. He saw all that happened as a part of God's plan for salvation.

Do you see God's bigger picture when he calls you to forgive?

Could someone else be watching whose salvation may be on the line, waiting for someone to show them something that the world doesn't possess? To see something from someone wise (like Joseph) who has a lot to teach and life-sustaining food to offer (like Joseph)? If we would believe it, we are spiritual Josephs. But of course, Joseph ultimately takes his cues from the other J-man: Jesus, the author and perfecter of our faith.

I think about Botham Jean's brother. What an amazing visual. If you're not familiar with the story, just do a search on that name. He's the man whose brother was shot and killed by an officer while relaxing in his own home. During the court proceedings, he let the officer know that he forgave her and asked if he could give her a hug. Forget about what Jesus would do (we already know), what would you do in that real-life situation? **Forgiveness is hard, but forgiveness is a must.**

I have a conviction about forgiveness, but I don't do it right all the time. It sounds hypocritical, but it's the truth. Still, I believe that without it, we won't see God. Some years back I was studying the Bible with a young man who shall remain nameless. At the time, we were thirsty for baptisms in this ministry. It was a dry time and this guy was interested! He so wanted to be baptized and I was so ready to baptize him, but something was holding him up. He had a tenuous relationship with his mother, and he couldn't bring himself to forgive her for the attitudes she held toward him or the wrong she'd done. As much as I wanted that baptism, I couldn't baptize him with a clear conscience.

We're still friends. I catch up with him and continue to pray for him. The fervor he once had has waned since then. Judge for yourself whether that was the right decision or not, but we need to ask: What sins do we prioritize over an unforgiving heart? Does sexual immorality come first? Lying? Theft?

The Big Picture

There's much in this to think over. I pray that God moves our hearts to see his big picture. Forgiveness is not about "freeing ourselves" as the world defines it, but rather tying ourselves to one another as soon as repentance has begun. As the father of the prodigal son sits on the edge of his seat waiting for his son's return, we should be yearning to forgive and be reconciled to one another. This is how the world will see a distinctive, Jesus kind of love (John 13:34–35). This is how we will be one together and in God (John 17:20–23).

Some Things to Consider

1. Would your friends, family, and sisters and brothers in the church consider you to be merciful?

2. How often are you willing to forgive someone?

3. Have you considered how much God has forgiven you?

4. Considering that forgiveness is a command, not a suggestion, how could you improve upon showing mercy as a part of your practical repentance?

8

A Relationship Where Confession Is Safe

And the prayer offered in faith will make the sick person well; the Lord will raise them up. If they have sinned, they will be forgiven. Therefore confess your sins to each other and pray for each other so that you may be healed. The prayer of a righteous person is powerful and effective.

—James 5:15–16

Confessing sin is central to any close and effective discipling relationship. Period.

But do you feel safe?

You should because of God, not exactly because of the other person involved.

Alex Jackson helped us so much in going deeper to understand the value of being vulnerable as the heart condition we need to get to this point. Let's see how he shares more in depth, as we consider the how and why we confess to one another.

A Confession about the Doctor

I have a confession. I despise going to the doctor's office. The semi-sterile atmosphere, the short, terse interactions, and facing vulnerable areas of my life with strangers isn't easy. Not to mention facing a difficult situation while sick or hurt. As if depending on someone else for help wasn't already difficult enough, Lord help us! But I know I need to go to the doctor, so I do it. With hesitancy and much reservation, I go.

I know this mindset of how I feel about going to the doctor is how many people approach confession. For some, there may even be stronger feelings because of abuse in our past. These feelings breed tension, avoidance, and often shame. But I know this was never God's intention. This chapter will build upon previous ones and look at how to redefine confession.

What Hinders Confession

As with all godly things, there is opposition to confession. While many people find that what hinders vulnerability also hinders confession, there is an added connotation of judgment. When Christians or people of faith think of confession there is a clear train of thought that leads to shame and regret.

But unlike a relationship with a doctor, who is an obvious authority, we are all at the same place at the foot of the cross, so there should NOT be a connotation of shame before one another. While you are likely to feel shame if you haven't acted as the doctor advised, most people take it at face value as doctor's advice. The opportunity to confess sin before one another is seen with much more weight. Yet the life that Christ asked of us is to be in a relationship with one another and helping one another. Look at James 5:13-16:

> Is anyone among you in trouble? Let them pray. Is anyone happy? Let them sing songs of praise. Is anyone among you sick? Let them call the elders of the church to pray over them and anoint them with oil in the name of the Lord. And the prayer offered in faith will make the sick person well; the Lord will raise them up. If they have sinned, they will be forgiven. Therefore confess your sins to each other and pray for each other so that you may be healed. The prayer of a righteous person is powerful and effective.
>
> Elijah was a human being, even as we are. He prayed earnestly that it would not rain, and it did not rain on the land for three and a half years. Again he

prayed, and the heavens gave rain, and the earth pro-duced its crops.

My brothers and sisters, if one of you should wander from the truth and someone should bring that person back, remember this: whoever turns a sinner from the error of their way will save them from death and cover over a multitude of sins (James 5:13–20).

In meditating on this passage I find it compelling that James notes that the elders' prayers are powerful, but so are each of ours! They help the troubled, give praise, and provide healing. Confession is just the prerequisite step. We are all called to be helping in the healing process of the entire church. For all of those who wanted to be in the medical profession but never went to school, this is your chance! Our position now is to help heal. Let Jesus pass his verdict in his time.

Why Do We Need Confession in Discipling Relationships?

From 1 John 1:10, we see that if we say we are without sin we call God a liar. God already knows the state of our hearts. So why is there such an emphasis on confession? For the most part, our confession is an opportunity to keep the clear, sober look of our lives and for us to connect with one another. All parties need agreement. Going to the doctor isn't of value if you walk away with no information or if your doctor doesn't get any information from you. What we do in our time with one another should be mutually beneficial.

In the chapter on vulnerability, we spoke about how openness and vulnerability breed trust.

This is definitely the first step to how God wants us to build deeper one-another relationships. But confession about sin specifically ties in accountability toward godliness; it is necessary in our quest to draw close to God. Could you imagine if none of your close relationships ended up in heaven? If the difference came down to them hearing the hard truth from someone they trusted and respected? This reminds me of a scripture:

I thank my God every time I remember you. In all my prayers for all of you, I always pray with joy because of your partnership in the gospel from the first day until now, being confident of this, that he who began a good work in you will carry it on to completion until the day of Christ Jesus...

God can testify how I long for all of you with the affection of Christ Jesus.

And this is my prayer: that your love may abound more and more in knowledge and depth of insight, so that you may be able to discern what is best and may be pure and blameless for the day of Christ (Philippians 1:3–10).

Here Paul's letter to the church in Philippi echoes his love and desire for them to grow to be like Jesus. This passage stands at the opening of Paul's letter and sets the tone for how he approaches God's people. If I have a one-another relationship for which I cannot see myself praying this prayer and echoing Paul's heart for partnership, affection, and help, then it's probably time for me to reevaluate why I have a relationship with that person at all.

How Can We Look at Confession Differently?

The average Christian will probably see by now that I have said nothing that you do not already know as truth. But it may be that God is calling us not to find a novel way to think about confession, but to practice it differently. I'm curious: if you were to stop and identify what the practice of confession has been like for you over the last five months, what patterns would you see? *Are you consistent?* Or is confession only at the dire moment when there is no other alternative? Do you see healing as others pray? When you confess, is it wholeheartedly or do you find yourself withholding something every time?

I have failed at every question above. I come from a deceptive and broken background where my greatest sin outside of pride is lying. I lied to get by to my friends. I lied to look good before my family. I lied to get and keep jobs. I lied to feel adequate before myself.

Confession, as John 3:19–21 states it, is coming into the light:

This is the verdict: Light has come into the world, but people loved darkness instead of light because their deeds were evil. Everyone who does evil hates the light, and will not come into the light for fear that their deeds will be exposed. But whoever lives by the truth comes into the light, so that it may be seen plainly that what they have done has been done in the sight of God.

The beauty of this passage is that it doesn't come with judgment, but shows that there is a place in life where you can be fully exposed before God and LIVE! With my lies, what I was ultimately seeking was approval. Can you relate? True approval is given by God when we live by the truth. And approval, when it's given by God, cannot be taken away.

I honestly believe one of the greatest aspects of confession, that goes undervalued, is taking the time to show people God's truth when they show us their brokenness. God gives us an opportunity to remind people of the light—the truth of his word. The truth that we are loved. The truth that there is no sin we commit before God that he didn't already know about. The truth that love is possible between two humans who were both broken. The truth that acceptance can be found within the church. The truth that you have value aside from what you accomplish. The truth that you are not what the world says you are. The truth that when we are most broken we can clearly see our need for Jesus.

More than any other, this passage in John 3:21 reminds me of the power of vulnerability, honesty, and strength. The writer reminds us that living by the truth is akin to living in the light, in full view of God. There is an echo here of what life could have been for us in the Garden of Eden, exposed yet not ashamed, vulnerable yet with full trust. We live a world desperate for vulnerability like never before but a world that is also fearful of the truth. It's through our relationships that we can offer people both.

Let's Build This Culture Again

Outside of the general culture of vulnerability, with confession we build a culture of facing faults and choosing Jesus. There are many other books that have great insights into this topic. In the area of building an atmosphere and relationship that fosters mutual confession, I strongly recommend reading *Golden Rule Leadership* by Gordon Ferguson and Wyndham Shaw. Just the first chapter gives a great set of principles and skills for how to have conversations with those in your community. The more we can live in truth, even in the face of our darkest moments, the more we will see God's character. Here are a few more practicals:

- *If you want to build trust, connect outside of confession times.*

- *Respect the privacy of anyone who shares with you and do not pass their information along unless they approve.*

- *Help those who confess to you to act on God's Scriptures as opposed to a fear of letting you down.*

Some Things to Consider

1. Would your friends, family, and brothers and sisters in the church consider you to be open about your sin? Or rather closed about your sin?

2. Do you confess the whole sin?

3. Do you realize it leads to powerful healing between you and God, and with your fellow brother or sister?

4. Considering that confession is a command, not a suggestion, how could you improve in opening up about sin as a part of your practical repentance?

9

A Relationship That Drives Repentance

My brothers and sisters, if one of you should wander from the truth and some-one should bring that person back, re-member this: Whoever turns a sinner from the error of their way will save them from death and cover over a multitude of sins.

—James 5:19–20

I always draw inspiration from how the letter from James ends. This is the type of repentance I hope to have—a repentance that saves and leads to powerful forgiveness from the Lord!

Yes, please.

Nathan Bigbee will offer us some great wisdom on how we can help each other continue to repent together. Repentance of course is individual, but many times, as we find in the Scriptures, repentance is corporate, and we need one another to fight against sin in our lives.

He will give us several considerations on how we can approach calling one another higher.

Overcoming Sin

In a perfect world we would only have to teach people how to live like Jesus and never deal with sin. Back to reality: sin exists, and when we train and help others to become like the Father we will have to deal with sin. And a lot of it! Helping people overcome sin and continuously be converted to Jesus is an amazing responsibility. Too many implement sloppy practices and can wind up doing more harm than good. Again, we are following Jesus, so let's look at how he discipled people to be like him!

Eager Patience

Jesus is serious about us repenting, and right away. In Matthew 5:23–24 he says, "If you are offering your gift at the altar and there remember that your brother or sister has something against you, leave your gift there in front of the altar. First go and be reconciled to them; then come and offer your gift." This has always been a scripture that challenges me.

The location of this sermon from Jesus makes the message all the more powerful. Jesus is speaking in Galilee. The person would have been offering their gift, an animal they either brought with them or bought there at the temple in Jerusalem. Going back to Galilee to reconcile and then returning would have been about a seven-day trip, effectively doubling their total travel time! They would have also needed to get another animal by that time. How inconvenient!

Jesus' point here is that before you come to get forgiveness from me, you need to go fix the issue that your brother or sister has against you. In other words, don't come to me acting like everything is OK and you are repenting when you aren't at peace with other members of my family. We need to help people to resolve sin quickly with one another.

One of the most common complaints from those who leave the church is other people. Many times that can be an excuse; however, bitter roots that go unresolved have caused many to walk away from both God and his church.

On the other hand, "the Lord is not slow to fulfill his promise as some count slowness, but is patient toward you, not wishing that any should perish, but that all should reach repentance" (2 Peter 3:9 ESV). Thank God! In fact, God is extremely patient with us when it comes to repentance. He warned and gave the Israelites time to repent for generations of people! We need to be patient with people and their repentance as well, provided their sin isn't harming others.

I'm so glad my wife has been patient with me. I am selfish. I didn't realize how much until we were engaged. Two weeks before we were married, we were advised to consider postponing the wedding because of how selfish I was. That kicked me into gear and I furiously repented. We wound up getting married at our originally planned date, but six months later my selfishness reared its ugly head again. I was loving my wife in the way that was comfortable and natural to me instead of the way she wanted to be loved. I had to furiously repent again. Over the years that story has continued and I've had to continuously grow and become more like Jesus in my selflessness. I'm so grateful that both my amazing wife and God are patient with my repentance.

There's a bit of a give-and-take here. On one side of the scale we need to urge people to drop everything to get right with God and others. We also need to refrain from getting impatient or frustrated when they take time or the change is slower than ideal.

Our Response Depends on Theirs

A fascinating Bible study is how Jesus responds to sin and confession from different individuals. All sin is against God. However, we do ourselves and those we are trying to help a major disservice when we have only one response to sin. I love to build things. I loved woodworking growing up and wound up studying civil engineering in college. When I graduated, I started out with just a drill and a handheld circular saw. With those two tools there was a limited number of things I could build. I have tried to use a drill to put in a nail before because I didn't have a hammer. FAIL!

The same is true when we try to help people with sin. If you only have one response, then you won't be able to help many people, and many times you will do more damage than good! Unfortunately, many of us respond based on our own internal scale of how bad we believe the sin to be instead of the condition or state of the sinner. Jesus didn't have just one response every time to sin. In fact, he responded differently to the same sin depending on several factors. One of the most important was the condition of the heart of the person he was helping.

We generally find out about sin in one of three ways: we witness it, another person tells us, or the individual opens up about it. For the same sin, those three ways of finding out should elicit different responses. Ultimately that boils down to their heart, which really comes out when we listen and ask questions. A sinner's heart usually lands in one of three categories or a combination of them: open, hard, or broken. Someone with an open heart is eager, humble, indignant, ready to change, open to advice, and asks questions, ready to do anything and everything to make things right. The hard-hearted person is stubborn, proud, shallow, self-righteous, arrogant, usually caught, and either unwilling to change or will only do so on their own terms. The broken individual is discouraged, heavyhearted, and feels bad about the sin but doesn't know how to change or feels like they can't. So how do we respond to these different hearts?

The Open Heart

As Jesus is teaching to a crowd of people, the Pharisees decide to test him by bringing a woman caught in adultery (John 8:3). I imagine she is embarrassed and humiliated, being made to stand before Jesus and crowds of people whom she would see as better than herself. Jesus does not condemn her; his only correction is, "Go now and leave your life of sin" (John 8:11). Not only that, but he shuts up those who wanted to make sure she gets what she deserves. 1 Corinthians 5:9–13 makes a strong plea for removing members of the church who are immoral. I wholeheartedly believe that there is a need to remove people from the church for being immoral, based on this scripture.

However, it takes a lot of wisdom and really depends on the condition of the sinner. In 1 Corinthians it seems that the man who is immoral is in an ongoing and unchanging relationship, and with his stepmother! Jesus gives grace to the woman caught in adultery, and an opportunity to change. Why? I believe because of her attitude and heart. The Scriptures don't comment on her condition, but the sense I get is remorse and readiness to change as she stands before her accusers.

It's heartbreaking when anyone sins, and sadly I've had quite a few people open up about being immoral. My response is always (to the best of my ability) based on their heart. Do they want to change or are they content with their sin? Are they humble and open to being radical about changing or reluctant and defensive? Did they open up voluntarily or did they try to hide their sin? I've corrected, rebuked, encouraged, and uplifted all for the same sin.

Luke 7:36–50 gives us an incredible picture of a woman who came totally repentant and ready to change. She's known in the city as a sinner, and there's a good chance she is an adulteress. She comes so ready to change that Jesus simply lifts her up as an example of repentance. In fact, the only thing he tells her is, "Your sins are forgiven" (verse 48) and "Your faith has saved you; go in peace" (verse 50). When someone is truly repentant and ready to change, they don't need another correction, but instead a "Great, let's move on to new heights in Jesus!"

The Hard Heart

Hearts can be hard for a moment, as with the apostles in Mark 6:52, or it can be a longer-term situation, as with the Pharisees (Matthew 23:27–28). Jesus' response to the woman at the well in John 4 is very interesting. Here is a woman who doesn't confess her sin when Jesus provides the opportunity by telling her to "go, call your husband and come back" (John 4:16). Women usually came in groups to the well. Most likely her public shame from the number of husbands she had was the reason she came alone.

Her response to Jesus asking for water is to question how he can ask, because Jews and Samaritans don't associate with one another. She then questions whether Jesus is who he says he is, due to a misunderstanding about the water he can provide. She is even skeptical and possibly derisive toward Jesus. His response is straightforward and punchy, almost a drop-the-mic moment. It's a stronger correction than he gives the woman caught in adultery. Yet he doesn't yell and gives her an opportunity to respond. How do you respond to someone caught in immorality, something God says is grounds for removal from his family?

One of the strongest responses from Jesus is toward one of his three closest friends, Peter. "Get behind me, Satan! You are a stumbling block to me; you do not have in mind the concerns of God, but merely human concerns" (Matthew 16:23). I imagine there were a few moments of silence after Jesus said this. What a gut punch! Peter had just told Jesus that he wouldn't go to the cross and essentially that he knew better than Jesus. He was arguing and tempting the Messiah, and Jesus would not have it (Matthew 16:21–22).

Jesus' responses to both Peter and the woman at the well are sharp and edgy, yet it's exactly what they needed to repent. In our age this kind of response is taboo, as our progressive society teaches us to accept and condone sinful behavior. We need men and women to stand up for what is right and teach and train hard hearts with tough, straight talks. When we shy away from these conversations, we do as much harm as when we are too harsh with the brokenhearted.

The Broken Heart

Many people I've worked with over the years have been in this boat. In fact, Satan tried to get Jesus down. Among Satan's most powerful weapons are doubt and persistent guilt. At the beginning of Jesus' ministry Satan tempts him while he is in the desert (Matthew 4; Luke 4). On a preliminary reading, it seems that there are three topics Satan tries to tempt Jesus with.

However, there is a fourth that is brought up with each overt temptation. Each temptation starts with "If you are the Son of God" (Matthew 4:3, 6; Luke 4:9). And this just after God has said, "This is my Son, whom I love; with him I am well pleased" (Matthew 3:17). If Satan tried to get Jesus to question his sonship with God, how much more will he try to get us to doubt? Satan loves for us to be in a place of doubt and discouragement. In order to repent, the broken soul needs to be lifted up, encouraged, and reminded where their citizenship lies, who they belong to, and how much he loves them!

Romans 3:9–18 gives us a clear picture of how God sees our sin. We are all utterly helpless and in great need! So how do we help one another overcome? Romans 3:20 says that "through the law we become conscious of our sin." There are many sins listed in the Scriptures, and we need to have deep convictions about them being wrong in our lives. However, a dead horse has never been set free from death by getting beaten more! Identifying sin and understanding its wickedness plays an essential role in our repentance. But when someone is convicted and broken by their sin already, why do we ask them to continue to study out how their sin is wrong?

Do not mishear me! We absolutely need to call people to stop sinning and gain a conviction about it, and write God's words on their heart. But remember, the goal is to help one another become like Jesus. **The goal is NOT to NOT sin.**

That leads to a life of neutrality that eventually slips back into sin. Once we are convicted that our sin is wrong, we must move on to replacing that sin with the righteous life that God requires. As we counsel, teach, and train we need to make sure that we aren't the ones pushing more guilt onto already guilty and broken souls. There is a caveat here about those who have worldly sorrow or falsely appear to be broken to appease people. More often than not, though, someone who has been in sin and has a guilty conscience constantly beats themselves up. We need to be quick to recognize an already broken soul, give grace, and point them to righteousness. **If we don't, we aren't really loving our brother and sister!**

Years ago a brother who had just been confronted about his pride in his dating relationship and life in general moved into the ministry I led. Although he really wanted to repent, he was having a difficult time doing so and moving forward. We got together, and I asked him if he had studied out pride, arrogance, and selfishness. He said that he had. I asked him how he felt about those things. He communicated that he was convicted about his own life and how wrong he had been.

He was shocked by my next response. I said, "Great! Then I want you to stop studying out those things. If you realize that they are wrong, hurting God and others, then studying them out more isn't going to help you. Instead I want you to study out and become humble and selfless." The shift of focus for him was exactly what he needed to be free and finally become like Jesus!

I had a similar experience myself. A year earlier I wasn't doing very well in several areas of my life. On my own accord I had come up with a list of character sins that I was embarrassed about. I called my discipler and let him know in brief how I was feeling. He wanted me to come over right away, even though I was supposed to give a lesson later that evening and needed to finish preparing.

I kissed my wife goodbye, told her I expected to be fired, and apologized to her. I went over to his house with my list in hand for reference. I started reading it to him, and he stopped me and asked if he could see it. My stomach dropped as I decided to hand it over, because I couldn't filter what was written down. He looked it over and said, "OK, do you need this anymore?" I stuttered and mentioned something about there being a Scripture reference on it. He asked if I remembered it, and I confirmed that I did. What happened next I will never forget: he ripped my list up into pieces and said, "I have been where you are before and sinned in most of these areas as well. But a list like this doesn't help anyone."

I. Lost. It. I started crying and felt so free for the first time I had in a long while! Do you set people free who are beaten down?

There is only one tool that works for every situation. That's God's word acting out love in its various forms. As disciples serving disciples, we need to know how to respond and *help* instead of react and hurt. That means much prayer, discernment, advice, and patience as we work with those God has entrusted us to help.

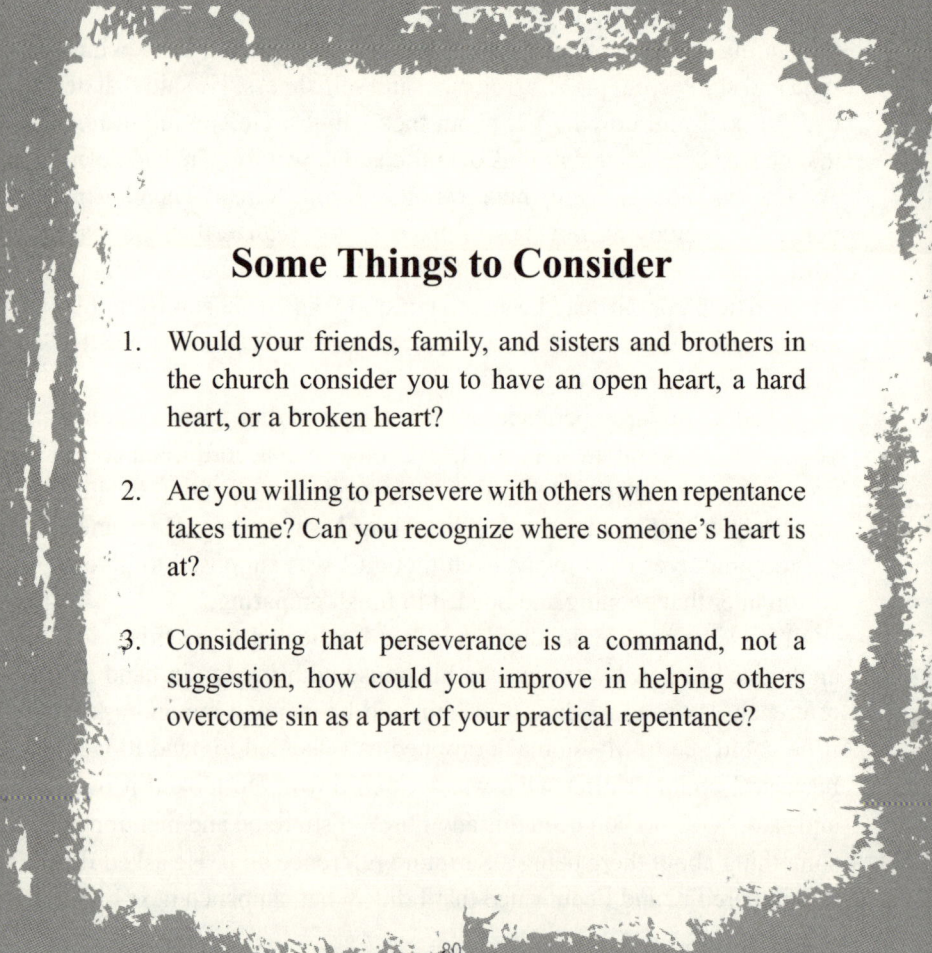

Some Things to Consider

1. Would your friends, family, and sisters and brothers in the church consider you to have an open heart, a hard heart, or a broken heart?

2. Are you willing to persevere with others when repentance takes time? Can you recognize where someone's heart is at?

3. Considering that perseverance is a command, not a suggestion, how could you improve in helping others overcome sin as a part of your practical repentance?

1. Carson, D. A., The Gospel According to John, in *The Pillar New Testament Commentary* (Leicester, England; Grand Rapids, MI: InterVarsity Press; W.B. Eerdmans, 1991), 217.

2. Carson, 220.

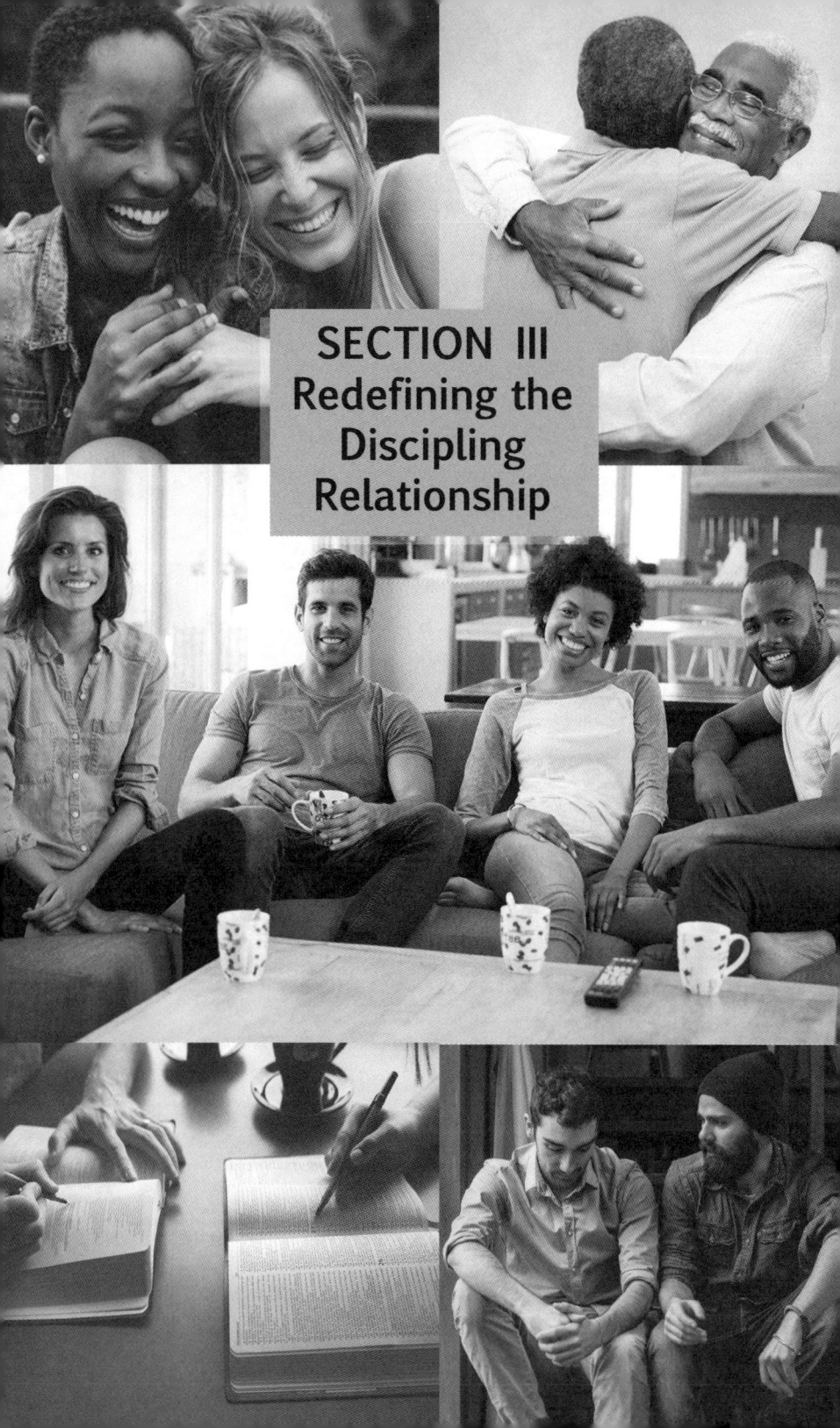

SECTION III
Redefining the Discipling Relationship

🔟 A Relationship Commended by the Lord

This is how we know what love is: Jesus Christ laid down his life for us. And we ought to lay down our lives for our brothers and sisters.

—1 John 3:16

Nafiisah Renshaw kicks off this final section of the book as we combine the principles from previous chapters to see our one-another relationships as a whole. She will guide us to take a look at what the discipling relationship can be at its fullest potential: when we strike the balance of really caring for one another, while at the same time keeping it real about the issues that arise in every family.

Caring for One Another

Practicing patience and kindness toward each other and striving not to dishonor one another will help us to always care for one another and build each other up. To care, according to the Oxford Dictionary, means:

- *to feel concern or interest; attach importance to something;*
- *to look after and provide for the needs of*

To care for the person God has entrusted to us for a time is to not just ask, "Did you read your Bible? Did you pray? What sin do you need to confess this week?" To care is to ask, in all sincerity, "How are you doing?"

Ask yourself these questions:

- Am I truly interested in the life and spiritual destiny of the person I'm discipling, or am I only interested in being able to tell my church leader that I met with that person?

- Is the time that I spend with my spiritual sister or brother important, or do I see our time together as a burden and a waste of time?

- Am I looking after my sister's or brother's spirit and soul? Are they looking after mine?

- Am I praying for them on a regular basis? Do they even come to mind?

This is of course not to say that every aspect of someone else's life is our concern, but consider Philippians 2:3–11.

Building Each Other Up

Part of caring for a fellow disciple is to be mindful in how we disciple each other. In 1 Thessalonians 5:14–15 Paul gave the disciples in the church at Thessalonica instructions on how to respond to their spiritual sisters and brothers going through different struggles. It's a very brief set of instructions, but if you think about it, very profound.

When we're discipling someone, do we pause to reflect on what they need from us? Do they need admonishment, comfort, encouragement, help, compassion, patience, or something else? Do they need us to pray with them rather than try to "fix" them or their situation? If it's a person who is continuing to struggle with the same sin, are they being prideful? Are they being stubborn? Are they being lazy? Are they feeling deeply insecure and not sure of themselves?

Let us be guided by the scripture above in how to respond, with the goal being to care for people and to build them up (1 Thessalonians 5:10–11), not tear them down. Let us also not forget that God is the one that brings about repentance, and for whatever reason he's allowing our sister or brother in Christ to struggle.

Trust his plan! He has deemed it necessary for their struggles to exist (Hebrews 5:8–9).

Paul warns the disciples in Galatia about biting and devouring one another, and in doing so ruining each other (Galatians 5:13–18). Later in his letter he called the spiritual disciples in Galatia to restore those who were weak (Galatians 6:1–2). As we disciple one another, one of our goals should be to not ruin each other, but to help each other grow spiritually strong and make it to heaven (Hebrews 3:12–14).

That may sound like a given, but let's be real…

How many times have we said or done something out of selfishness and pride, not considering other people at all? Most likely multiple times. Pausing to reflect on each of our discipling relationships to gain a sober judgment of the relationship and of ourselves in that relationship is important (Romans 12:1–3).

Sometimes We All Need to Be Rebuked

There will be times when we're trying to help a fellow disciple who seemingly refuses to repent. In those times we should turn to Matthew 18:15–17 for guidance. In that passage, Jesus teaches about what to do to restore our struggling sister or brother in Christ. We are to talk to them one on one, then bring one or two others in if needed, then bring in the church as a last resort.

Nowhere in Jesus' instruction or anywhere else in the Bible are we told to condemn our spiritual sister or brother to hell, talk down to them, or make them feel like a terrible person. However, the Bible does direct us to tell the truth, calling each other to see God's way and his righteousness (again, Matthew 18:15–17). It's our responsibility as disciples to have conversations with one another about our sins, to show each other scriptures, and to remind each other of what God calls us to do.

We need to share with one another what God expects of us and to say plainly, with love and respect, that if there's no repentance the day will come when God will just give us over to our sinful nature (Romans 1:18–32). When that day comes, we are going to have to suffer the consequences in a profound way (Romans 2:1–16). Take heart; Scripture teaches us that there is hope for repentance, that we do not have to continue in our sin, that we have been set free (Romans 6:15–23). We want all people to be saved (1 Timothy 2:1–4), just as

God does, but he allows us all to have free will and to make our own decisions.

Circling Back

We have got to approach every discipling time knowing that discipleship is a relational process; it's a marathon, not a sprint, as they say. No one is a sinner in need of God's grace one moment, and the next perfect and free from sin as Christ was. We will never achieve perfection in the sense of being free from all flaws, but we can help each other be perfect, whole and complete, not lacking in anything (James 1:2–4).

Some Things to Consider

1. Would your friends, family, and brothers and sisters in the church consider you to be caring?

2. Do you feel built up by others?

3. Or do you feel torn down by others?

4. Considering that building one another up is a command, not a suggestion, how could you improve in it as a part of your practical repentance?

11

A Relationship=
A Friendship

My command is this: Love each other as I have loved you. Greater love has no one than this: to lay down one's life for one's friends.

—John 15:12-13

Friendship or Relationship? Or Both?

One common discussion we have heard is that you can be in a discipling relationship, even if you are not close friends with the other person. It's not the ideal situation, but it can occur. The ideal is to be close friends or grow into being close friends.

But how does this happen?

In John 15:15 Jesus said to the Twelve that by that point they were his friends, and he wanted them to have a more intimate understanding of God the Father. You could pose that if we are to imitate Jesus in this with those we are in discipling relationships with, then it is imperative that we learn to build real friendship in order to have that intimate connection in our one-another relationships.

So let's look at a couple of the authors of this book who happened to become the best of friends over eleven years prior to this writing. These two brothers started out as acquaintances, but the Lord brought about a closeness that has grown and is still growing till this day.

Sitting at the Master's Feet

I (Nate) moved to San Antonio in 2008 with the dream of being trained to serve in the full-time ministry by expert builders. There was no promise of a job in San Antonio, only that I would be trained for the ministry if that was what I wanted. Shortly before I moved, Hervé Fleurant called me and asked if I'd like to be an intern. I said yes, and our now eleven-year friendship was on its way. What surprised me when I first moved here was that training didn't look quite like I expected it to. I was ready for method, books to read, a program, steps, etc. All those things came over the years, but our relationship was the focus. How we spend our time really shows what we believe in, our interests, and how we invest.

"Discipling time" always started at the dinner table with the family on Tuesdays at 6 pm. After dinner we headed into the living room and watched a basketball game with the whole family (I frequently fell asleep during the game). Finally, around 10 pm we went into the office to talk through ministry issues. After we had done this for about a year, Chris jumped into the picture. We would have dinner, watch a game or Avatar: The Last Airbender, and then talk shop in the office. Hervé (whom we nicknamed "Uncle") invested a lot of time into both of us. Spending that much time with him and the family that wasn't about "talking ministry" built a solid foundation of trust for Chris and me. Food bonds, it's as simple as that. Consider Jesus and food:

John 2:1–10	Wedding feast: turned water to wine, kicked off ministry, performed first miracle
Luke 5:27–39	Ate with tax collectors and sinners, called sinners to repent
Luke 6:1–5	Defended his disciples eating grain on the Sabbath, taught about the Sabbath
Luke 7:36–50	Ate at Simon the Pharisee's house and taught about gratitude
Mark 6:32–44	Fed 5000 men and more women and children
Mark 8:1–9	Fed 4000 men and more women and children
Luke 11:37–54	Corrected Pharisees at a Pharisee's house

Luke 14:1–24   Healed and told parables at chief Pharisee's house

John 12:1–11   At Simon the Leper's, rebuked disciples as Mary
                anointed him

John 13:1–38   The Last Supper, final moments before his death

Luke 24:28–32 He reappeared to some of the disciples then
                disappeared!

Luke 24:41–49 Explained what had happened and what would
                shortly happen next

John 21:1–23   Restored Peter

Jesus spent a good amount of time over a meal with the disciples, those he was trying to convert, the multitudes, and even his enemies. Hearts were moved, repentance was initiated and brought to completion, people were taught and rebuked, and vision was instilled, all over meals! Even science is now proving that eating together promotes closeness with one another. That was the real start of deepening Chris's and my relationship. The first time we met was at a taco restaurant. We ate and got deep quickly with one another. It sparked in us a brotherhood that has kept us close for the last decade.

Being at the dinner table with Hervé and watching the way he interacted with his family and being a part of it was priceless. Now don't get me wrong. Paul told Timothy, "The things you have heard me say in the presence of many witnesses entrust to reliable people who will also be qualified to teach others" (2 Timothy 2:2). Training in the traditional sense is crucial, and we needed that from Hervé as well, just as Jesus gave on many occasions. But that foundation of family time together molded and bonded us in a way that was undeniably important for us.

We live in a dangerous age, though. Adults are spending around eleven hours a day consuming media of some sort. We get far more screen time than we do facetime. Many dinner times where the family used to connect have been replaced with connection to the internet. We communicate more with our thumbs than with our mouths. All this leads to distrust, disconnect, and a lack of real relationship. The one-another relationships we are striving to get back to cannot take place on our screens!

On top of this, there is a strong and unhealthy disconnect between the younger and older generations. "Young bucks" should be sitting at the feet of a master and eagerly learning, just as the pupils of rabbis did in Jesus' time. It saddens me when I hear about the younger generation waiting for the older to let go of the reins. Instead we ought to be like Elisha, who followed Elijah right until he died (2 Kings 2). Or David who waited patiently for fifteen or twenty years for a tyrant to be removed before becoming king (1 Samuel 15; 2 Samuel 5). The reality is that David realized that this was God's timing and not his. The same is true for us today! Chris and I were shaped by the time we spent with Hervé face to face and among his family.

Do you spend time outside of just "going over the checklist"?

The deep conversation and training late at night were crucial as well. Timothy and Titus (albeit not at the same time) sat at the feet of Paul and learned from him. We had the unique experience of both being able to sit at the feet of a master at the same time, and that created a real depth of relationship. Both of us sitting at the feet of a master builder, learning how to raise a family and having deep conversation late at night, was the foundation Chris and I both needed to move us forward.

A Flash of Paul ➥ Timothy and Titus

I (Chris) moved to San Antonio, Texas in 2009. As Nate recapped how we first met one another and our mentorship under Hervé, I couldn't help but reflect that our relational bond developed all within about one year that God blessed us to experience. Even if we don't think it's possible, God can do amazing things in a very short time… Some of us, like me in 2009, may not at all fathom a best friend (Nate) and a spiritual mentor (in this case Uncle Hervé) being added to their life in only one year. Wow. When I moved to San Antonio, my mindset was to complete a dispatch assignment for my company. It was my sole priority. In no way did I see that God had a bigger, better plan for my life.

Fast forward to 2020. Nate and I have continued to grow closer over the years even though we live in different cities. We both still regularly consider the learning from Hervé, and still continually seek his counsel for various life situations. In 2009, we were both single young men, likened to Timothy and Titus learning under Paul. Today, we are both happily married husbands, lucky to have amazing wives. We are both fathers of sons and daughters. We still connect to help one another be better husbands and fathers via Christ's instructions. Amid all these life stages, we both often reflect on how we watched, learned, and are now imitating the qualities of Christ we received firsthand sitting in Uncle's house. We watched and still see his example of being a servant to his wife, his children, his family, and the church. And now, a decade later, we strive to imitate his example of Christ. Examples like his are a flash of Paul to Timothy and Titus, and the legacy we can all leave when we take others under our own wing to help build them in Christ. Nate and I both can say with sincerity, *"We are eternally grateful to God for allowing us to have an uncle such as Hervé is to us."*

Fighting and Relaxing Together

One of the things I admire about Jesus is that he did everything with his disciples. Some of us just hang out, others just get down to brass tacks. Jesus was with the disciples as they went through hardships and as they enjoyed each other's company. Soon after Chris and I met, we started studying the Bible with a teen. It was a tag-team experience, and I came to appreciate and love the way Chris thought and how we balanced each other on the "battlefield." Proverbs 17:17 says, "A friend loves at all times, and a brother is born for a time of adversity" (ESV). There is something about being in the fight and going through battles together that transforms us into true sisters and brothers. Chris and I became so close that we wound up calling each other "wonder twins."

One of the things I appreciate most about Chris is how deep he is. Our talks can go on for hours, and I love it! What's interesting, though, is that although we both love being deep, we often don't agree on topics when we get started. We come from different spiritual and cultural backgrounds. Even the way we've been taught in God's kingdom is often not the same. However, I always feel like I can disagree and continue the conversation because I know how much love Chris has for me and that he respects me. Without this, I know

I would have walked away feeling salty after a good number of our discussions.

And the truth is that although we come from different backgrounds, we have Christ in common, which should trump everything else!

> *In Christ Jesus you are all children of God through faith, for all of you who were baptized into Christ have clothed yourselves with Christ. There is neither Jew nor Gentile, neither slave nor free, nor is there male and female, for you are all one in Christ Jesus* (Galatians 3:26–28).

This is crucial! Especially so in our current racial and political climate. Because we have put on Christ, nothing else should come between us. As soon as it does, Jesus is no longer as important as our issues, backgrounds, or opinions. Love not only covers over a multitude of sins, but also a plethora of ideas and viewpoints.

Consider these scriptures (emphasis mine):

> 1 Corinthians 1:10: *I appeal to you, brothers and sisters, in the name of our Lord Jesus Christ, that all of you* agree with one another in what you say *and that there be* no divisions among you, *but that you be* perfectly united in mind and thought.

> 1 Peter 3:8 ESV: *Finally, all of you, have* unity of mind, *sympathy, brotherly love, a tender heart, and a humble mind.*

> Acts 4:32 *ESV: Now the full number of those who believed were of* one heart and soul, *and no one said that any of the things that belonged to him was his own, but they had everything in common.*

> Philippians 2:1–2 ESV: *So if there is any encouragement in Christ, any comfort from love, any*

*participation in the Spirit, any affection and sympathy,
complete my joy* by being of the same mind, having
the same love, being in full accord and of one mind.

God wants us to be united and agree with one another! The only way that can happen is by loving each other and making the Scriptures our standard. I get concerned anytime I hear that someone has no relationships, because Christ has ceased to be the standard for their life. It's more of an issue of their relationship and obedience to God than it is about their ability to bond. Again, if we have Christ, then we have every ability and reason to connect with other disciples.

The spiritual fight is important to our relationships, but so is rejuvenation. The practice of resting is making a comeback in our family of churches. One of my fondest memories with Chris was out at a river in the hill country just outside San Antonio. There was a rope swing that hung from a fifty-foot limb. We used to head out there and barbeque and have a blast on the swing. I decided to attempt what the locals called the "fall from heaven." I climbed up the tree to where the fifty-foot limb was and after much deliberation, jumped. The fall didn't go well, and let's just say that I was fairly convinced I was bleeding because of the impact.

Without hesitation Chris jumped right in the water and helped me back to shore. I was fine, but I appreciate so much his instantaneous concern for me. After getting plenty more Texas sun that day, we headed home with the windows rolled down, blaring Purple Rain and singing along. I know Jesus probably didn't swing on a rope swing, but he had defining moments of not only rest but also spiritual rejuvenation with his disciples.

If there's one moment in the Scriptures that I would love to watch or be a part of, it's when Jesus took Peter, James, and John up on the mountain to witness the transfiguration. The truth is that Jesus was frequently outdoors, spending time in God's creation with his closest friends. For me being in the mountains, hills, and rivers is where I spiritually recharge. Years later Chris and I went hiking together, and it was another defining moment for us. We hiked, prayed, and dreamed of the future.

Not everyone likes the outdoors, but spending time together

doing things we love is important to our relationships. Without those times, our relationships can start to feel like appointments, and then just business. Jesus was balanced, and God has blessed Chris and me with an incredible brotherhood that I feel exemplifies what he wants our relationships to look like.

Planning a Future Together

A final consideration of Jesus' example is how he always helped the disciples see the vision. He led them to see God's plan for their whole lives with the Holy Spirit—a plan for them to overcome sin in their own lives, impact the world, and live a life worthy of the calling. Whenever Nate and I had our adventures together, we often went deep, discussing where our lives were and where we were going from there.

Nate mentioned a hike in 2018 at Government Canyon in the Texas Hill Country. On that hike, he revealed to me some of his deepest challenges and struggles. I did the same. We opened up about battling depression, having relapses in purity, and common struggles in our young marriages as we both were learning to be better husbands, not to mention first-time fathers. In that environment we were both free to talk without judgment, trusting and knowing the other was there for full support. It was a great hike but a hard time emotionally too, as we both had failures and letdowns in life. We also had quite a deal of successes to celebrate, but the enemy is always on the attack.

That hike culminated in a prayer that I have not forgotten since. Nate prayed for me, and I for him. We decided to intercede on behalf of one another that day in a deliberate manner. Even though we were both humbled and sobered by confessions, God lifted our spirits as we hiked out from the canyon. It marked a time of discipling, but for me, a time of deep friendship and brotherhood.

We continue to look forward together, as Paul noted in Philippians 3. Our brief, eleven-year relationship has been marked with incredible encouragement and times of sorrow, yet we still dream about a future when our kids will call each other cousins, knowing uncle and auntie well. We plan to continue to be there for each other when times are hard, visit one another's homes, have family vacations together, go on more hikes, and even retire together, perhaps serving in some elder/shepherd role for a small church. This is the future we pray for and look to until one or both of us is called home.

Lord willing, here's to the next fifty years or so with my friend, growing into all things Christ.

Some Things to Consider

1. Are the people you are in discipling relationships with you good friends or becoming good friends?

2. Do you initiate friendship? Or do you wait for others to initiate it with you?

3. Considering that Jesus himself desired for the Twelve to be his friends, how can you change your approach to build more friendship?

1 2

A Relationship Bearing Fruit That Will Last

You did not choose me, but I chose you and appointed you so that you might go and bear fruit—fruit that will last—and so that whatever you ask in my name the Father will give you.
This is my command: Love each other.

—John 15:16-17

What do we believe God can do when the pieces of this loving-one-another puzzle, aka discipling, start to come together? With faith it is easier to see the "big" picture and have more clarity even if small pieces of the puzzle are still left out! Just consider this as the big picture:

An environment where people treat each other in the ways of love with deep conviction, sin is openly dealt with, and relationships are defined by trust and protection.

A few questions to pose about this ideal condition: Does this describe a hint of what the Lord Jesus meant when he said, **"A new command... By this all people will know that you are my disciples"**? (HCSB). If we were to break that down, what considerations about how we go about discipling relationships could we uncover? What are the implications about our evangelism? As we have heard a great deal in this book about redefining the one-another commands, redefining overcoming sin, and redefining the discipling relationship, let's deeply consider the fruit that can result from obeying the Lord's "new command."

BY THIS

By what again, Lord?... Exactly what is Jesus referring to? Naturally, we all know academically, right? He's referring to our love for one another (Chapters 2–5). But let us not be so quick to read over that simple point. Let us deepen our conviction once again, making a united effort to ensure that our relationships are characterized:

BY THESE	And Not by These
Patience	Hierarchy
Kindness	Harshness
Listening and Understanding	Quick Fixes
Trust as the Foundation	Structure as the Foundation
Service that Protects	Service to Control
Quality Time	Transactional D-time
Relationship	Process

Some of these items may raise the hair on the back of your neck, as I've heard that many of us in the past, including myself, have experienced some of the less-desired characteristics described above. The key is to not focus so much on the past hurts, but let us consider how we can move forward with renewed faith to make the change back to that new command. A quick and important note on structure, however. Structure is not bad. It is certainly needed, but it is not a priority over relationship. Our hearts will never be motivated by process alone. We need to be motivated by our love for one another. We need to be convicted by the Lord's example.

ALL PEOPLE

Who again, Lord?... You mean that *all* the people around us disciples could be impacted if we get that first part down? So "all" means not just other disciples, but it also refers to a larger crowd, the lost. Those who are spiritually wandering, the poor, the homeless, the prisoners, the addicts, the outcasts of our society. Yeah, those people. "All" would include our own family members, neighbors, classmates, and coworkers. Now this is all fine sounding, but how does it look practically? I'm sure by now in this book, this can be a burning question for many, and we do need to get there, but let's consider just a couple more words from Jesus. The key takeaway, however, is that there is a large human audience in this world waiting for our love.

WILL KNOW

Will know what, Lord?... Know that we are his. There is power in being redeemed, you know. So, by having true, loving one-another relationships, we can impact all the people in our lives with what again, exactly? It seems Jesus is making a fairly straightforward call to us when considering Matthew chapter 28's conclusion. He wants all people to know who we are, and more importantly, he wants all people to know we are his. The Lord Jesus seems to have a way of thinking here that our individual and relational behavior and culture, as a part of his body, has a great deal to do with how we are understood, or at least perceived, by the people around us.

What's the connection here to our evangelistic efforts? I'd pose this academic consideration:

The feasibility to impart a life-changing knowledge of Jesus is very low without clear evidence of powerful, loving relationships as the church culture.

Put quite frankly, it's hard to impact someone for Jesus if you don't have many close, real relationships around you in which love is obvious. To me at least, there is a direct correlation to how God can use us to spread the gospel of Christ and the quality of our one-another relationships. I'd almost go as far as saying you can't have one without the other.

Great evangelism is tough without great relationships.

Practical vs Faithful

With this, the question of practicality arises...again. Someone will say, as has been said many times over, "What does this look like?" Wow. It seems a common question nowadays. Especially when there is frustration about both: not-so-great discipling and not-so-great evangelism. One thought is that this is more related to our faith than we may expect. We'd like to skip to a fast, practical solution… NOW. It's quite the Western way when facing a problem. Solve it, and quickly please.

But maybe there is wisdom in having a bit of spiritual patience here—consider that faith born from the very words of Jesus can help us out yet again. Even if the message is "old," we've nonetheless spent most of this book striving to bring back that classic essence of Jesus and his word to rebuild faith in areas that have grown weak. We need both faith and action for sure. So here are a couple of quick takes on the age-old question: "What does all of this fine-sounding stuff look like?"

Take 1 – Ready, Get Set,…

If we really want to get practical about things, it is imperative to understand that we convert people to Christ via relationship, not process. And the practice of building relationships can be something especially challenging for us in the USA. This culture prides itself on individuality, quick action, and fast results. That is what many would consider the marks of American success. Not saying these are bad at the outset, but some of these qualities we are known for can prohibit the successful practice of relationship building. I have often over-looked the value in great understanding versus the value of instant results. This brings to mind a proverb: "A patient person shows great understanding."

When we ask the question, "What does this look like?" so quick-ly, we are literally mimicking our Western culture. "Jus' gimme the answer!" Joe or Sally may exclaim. Or is it that we get it (mentally at least) and just want clear instruction? Have we lost some of the patience that takes the time to inquire of the Lord? This kind of pa-tience could lead us to ask him, "What am I missing? What are we missing?" Or "God, can you help guide me again with your Holy Spirit here?"

Instead of the Western culture, I hope we can continue to build a spiritual culture that values our collective success—success defined not only by external results, but also by our state of being (our one-another relationships). Perhaps the first practical matter is to change our focus. First fix the internal, then the external will follow, as the Lord stated—love each other first: only then will all men know we are his. Besides, wasn't it the Lord himself acting via the Holy Spirit who added to their number daily when thousands were getting baptized in Acts chapter 2? Those disciples had their hearts and minds clearly devoted to God and to one another. Greatest commandment hand in hand with the second greatest commandment indeed.

Take 2 – GO!

Here's a practical story from my life that I've experienced over ten times in the past decade (roughly 2010–2020). The story is pretty much the same, but the names are different. Well, one name above all is the same, that's Jesus. In various circumstances, I was introduced to someone slowly and steadily. The Holy Spirit led the way for sure each time. Rarely did I invite these people to church upon first interaction. Most were simply my neighbors, a couple of classmates, and a couple of mentees. People who were around me at least once or twice a week if not daily. In each case, I prayed that God would create a strong friendship full of trust, a sense of realness, and just plain ol' "I got your back." Again, there was no rush in getting these folks to attend a church service or Bible talk, but there was a rush in introducing them to that consistent name of Jesus.

It starts with some conversation, not simply one conversation, but a nice handful over time, a month or two of interactions when the conversations start to get real. We talk about real issues of life, ups and downs, successes and failures. In those kinds of dialogues, the name of Jesus has plenty of opportunity to come up, either in praising him for bringing me success or in going to him in prayer because I'm struggling. Either way, his name is spoken. I mean, just being a disciple here. Nothing extraordinary. If you talk about life with a disciple of Christ, then his name is going to pop up naturally. I believe the Holy Spirit will ensure an itch in the person's ear. Marriage issues? Parenting concerns? Financial issues? Health challenges? This is life on this earth. Go to Jesus for all of it, good and bad.

I try to relate to the person and empathize, sharing how Christ has helped me in a life situation. Many times, I drop scriptures in passing in conversation without even opening the Bible. Perhaps the power of God's word is that potent that it attracts a person to ask each time, "Why Jesus?" in some shape, form, or fashion—and there it is! There's an opening from the Spirit.

And before you knew it, out of those Holy Spirit setups, a Bible study would burst forth, literally. The name of Jesus was firmly in place, and so was a real relationship. Both were present at the point of starting Bible studies. A little bit of patience goes a long way. It was clear to those ten or twelve individuals that this wasn't a church gimmick, nor was it an over-the-top religious experience to embark upon. It was for real.

So God has used me to baptize at least one person every year for the past ten years. Doesn't sound too impressive, and it's not, honestly. In my opinion it is minimum effort from a man. Still, I can't help but imagine a church where each member doing the same (literally each and every member converts one). That would mean churches would double in growth each year.

The Lord added to their number! Do we still believe this?

Now credit due. Each person I baptized came from a 100% Holy Spirit–driven situation. Rarely did I ever use cold contact, and in fact none of those I've baptized in the past decade were by the standard church invite. Not at all saying that inviting is bad! I've done it hundreds of times. Just saying I haven't baptized someone with that approach since I was in campus. When I was a college student it was my main approach, and sure, God used me to baptize several folks over my time in the campus ministry. But as a single, and now a married guy over the past ten years, not a one was from cold contact. Haven't been door-knocking in a long time.

I have invited folks on the random, a person I was sitting next to on an airplane or my waiter from Cheesecake Factory. I mean, by all external signs, my personal evangelism is a debacle, yet several people comment to me that I'm a super-evangelistic brotha! It's because of people consistently getting baptized, but that's not me! The reality is that I could really improve my evangelistic efforts quite a bit and in many ways, but God has used me due to just making a simple everyday effort to love people and build relationships.

Who will get the credit for ten baptisms? 100 baptisms? 1000 baptisms? Exactly. Human effort is not the point. In my strong opinion, if we set out with the goal in mind to love first, then the Lord will add to our growth as a church. What did Paul say again to the church in Corinth? It didn't matter who baptized them, it was all about gaining the knowledge of Christ. Our love for one another is the key to learning how to build excellent relationships. If we can't do it internally, it may be tough to do it externally with the world. There's a heavy practical for the leaders. Let's train ourselves to become expert relationship builders via discipling. (A toolkit and workshop guide is included in the appendix of this book that focuses primarily on how to train and mentor one another in this manner.)

So let's GO love one another deeply, cover over a multitude of sins, and become expert relationship builders! That is my best advice. Then we can GO make disciples of every nation. At least that's my personal story and takeaway from a brief decade in time.

Thanks for taking the time to read the thoughts my fellow sisters and brothers in Christ shared in this book. We hope you are reinvigorated by God's powerful word and the personal stories found in each chapter.

- *People are not converted to Christ via process, rather via love and relationship!*

- *We can redefine what discipling is all about.*

- *We can do it with the faith that is born from the words of Christ.*

- *A new command is at hand. Let's imitate and train that.*

- *Let's love one another deeply from the heart and see the Lord work powerfully in our lives!*

- *Amen.*

Epilogue

I just finished writing a short book entitled *The Power of Relationships*. The title of the last chapter in that book is, "My Hope Is in Our Youth." Those of the older generations among us, like me, have made our contributions to this movement of churches that we now call the ICOC. While we yet have contributions to make as individual disciples, the impact of our leadership has been diminishing consistently for some years. That fact is unmistakably shown in our growth statistics. We as a movement are all but stalled out. If the Great Commission is to have a significant impact on our lost world, the younger generations among us are going to be the ones God raises up to carry it out—and it cannot be carried out without the consistent application of discipling among all of God's children.

That realization makes me extremely grateful for this book written by those who are younger. Their idealism is still intact, and they will not entertain any thought of failing to change the world. They are determined that their lives will have a big impact on eternity. Jesus said that we must become like little children to enter the kingdom of heaven, and children are idealistic. As they enter early adulthood, they respond to challenges with hope. Hearing that something cannot be done or has never been done excites them. They think, "Good, I get to be the first!"

Discipling is the concept that most attracted me to what was often called the Discipling Movement in the 1970s and 1980s. It was the missing ingredient in the churches of which I had been a part and the missing ingredient in my own life. The subtitle of a book on the topic that I wrote back in 1997 was simply, "God's Plan to Train and Transform His People." That was the phrase suggested by my then-editor and still dear friend, Tom Jones, who wrote the foreword to this book, *Discipling Redefined.*

Being trained encompasses what it will take to become more like Jesus in his mission to seek and save the lost. Being transformed encompasses what it will take to become more like Jesus in his heart and character. If our lives reflect his great heart for people of all types and are spent in helping change the world one person at a time, we will come to the end of our days looking back with great satisfaction and gratitude for a life well spent.

At age seventy-seven, I am coming to the end of my life. I have many regrets and wish I had done many things differently. But one thing I will never regret is embracing the concept and practice of this thing we call discipling nearly four decades ago. It has changed my life and my eternity. May it change yours as well, and may this new book help it to do just that!

—Gordon Ferguson
McKinney, Texas

TRAINING●REDEFINED

Practical Guide

Then Jesus came to them and said, "All authority in heaven and on earth has been given to me. Therefore go and make disciples of all nations, baptizing them in the name of the Father and of the Son and of the Holy Spirit, and teaching them to obey everything I have commanded you. And surely I am with you always, to the very end of the age."
—Matthew 28:18–20

APPENDIX A-1: Embracing the Heart to Train
Figure 1.1 – Commands of Jesus: One-Another Umbrella
Figure 1.2 – One-Another Training Themes

APPENDIX A-2: Imitating Christlike Empathy
Figure 2 – The Empathy Pyramid

APPENDIX A-3: Imitating Christlike Mentoring
Figure 3.1 – Mentoring = [Nurture + Coach] Model
Figure 3.2 – Life Stage Group Discipling

APPENDIX B: One-Another New Testament Reference Study

Curriculum Introduction

Considering Matthew 28, the Lord wants us to teach disciples to obey all he has commanded in a continuous manner. This practical guide sets out to give an approach to helping disciples everywhere to train one another in the ways of Christ. The primary approach is focused on training that exists in a relationship defined by the "new command": love one another.

Chapters 1 through 12 of this book are intended to address the heart and highlight the principles of what the ideal relationship in Christ can be when disciples embrace the many aspects of loving one another as Jesus commanded. What chapters 1 through 12 do not clearly reveal, however, is:

How can we get there, practically speaking?

Thus, we wanted to provide training models that can support churches in creating and sustaining Christlike discipling practices. This practical guide has three core modules:

❶ Embracing the Heart to Train

❷ Imitating Christlike Empathy

❸ Imitating Christlike Mentoring

For each of these modules, we lay out a curriculum that is flexible enough to cover over a week, at a congregational midweek, at a small group, at a leader's meeting, or at your own personal speed. Each module has a curriculum structure that provides:

- Background
- Scriptural Focus
- A One-Another Model(s)
- Practical Instruction
- Group Discussion Points

We pray that however you may utilize this practical guide, it will be inspiring and enlightening. We pray and hope it will help disciples grow and help one another to become more and more like Jesus Christ our Lord. *That's the goal, after all: to continuously learn and imitate the Lord.* With this goal in mind, the church grows stronger:

> *Instead, speaking the truth in love, we will grow to become in every respect the mature body of him who is the head, that is, Christ. From him the whole body, joined and held together by every supporting ligament, grows and builds itself up in love, as each part does its work* (Ephesians 4:15–16).

Embracing the Heart to Train

Let the message of Christ dwell among you richly as you teach and admonish one another with all wisdom through psalms, hymns, and songs from the Spirit, singing to God with gratitude in your hearts. —Colossians 3:16

Background

When we consider Colossians 3:16, we must start by asking ourselves what is the "message of Christ" that we should utilize as a basis to teach and admonish one another? A primary perspective points to learning to love. Love God. Love each other. So if it starts there, how can we break that down? The model below is not all inclusive of the discipling focus, but it helps visualize just how many commands there are that instruct us how to love each other:

Figure 1.1 – Commands of Jesus: One-Another Umbrella – Colossians 3:14

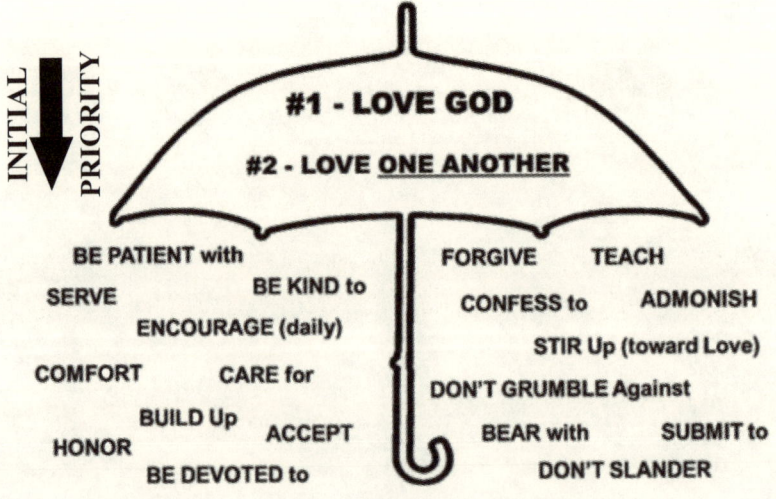

Scriptural Focus

➡ Bible study recommended for leader meeting or small group:

- **1 John 4:19–20** – Can we love God without excelling in loving one another?

- **1 John 3:21–24** – How committed are we to teaching these commands?

One-Another Model

➡ Consider the following model of four training focus areas derived from various one-another commands that we can teach and build deep conviction upon:

Figure 1.2 – One-Another Training Themes (House)

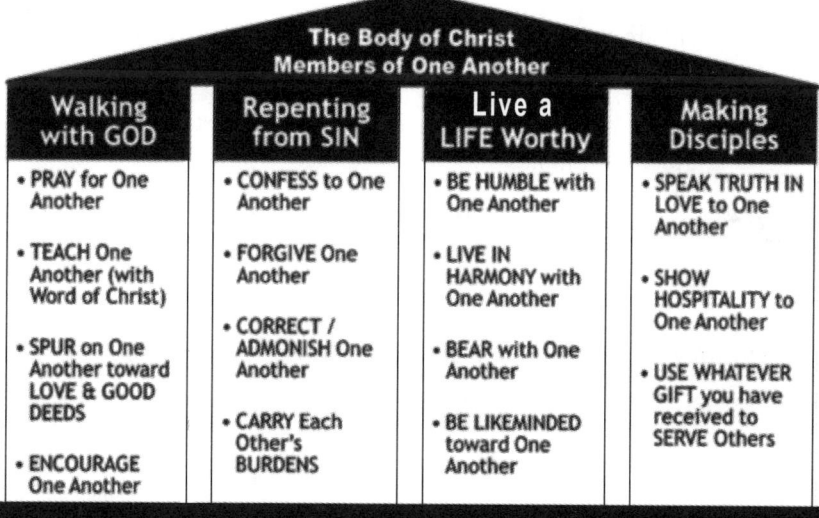

Walking with GOD	Repenting from SIN	Live a LIFE Worthy	Making Disciples
• PRAY for One Another	• CONFESS to One Another	• BE HUMBLE with One Another	• SPEAK TRUTH IN LOVE to One Another
• TEACH One Another (with Word of Christ)	• FORGIVE One Another	• LIVE IN HARMONY with One Another	• SHOW HOSPITALITY to One Another
• SPUR on One Another toward LOVE & GOOD DEEDS	• CORRECT / ADMONISH One Another	• BEAR with One Another	• USE WHATEVER GIFT you have received to SERVE Others
• ENCOURAGE One Another	• CARRY Each Other's BURDENS	• BE LIKEMINDED toward One Another	

The Body of Christ — Members of One Another

Discipling built upon: LOVE ONE ANOTHER

Practical Instruction

1. Identify one or two areas of improvement for yourself individually from the model above.

2. Discuss with close relationships ideas of how to grow in that improvement area.

3. Discuss within small groups each training area topic over one or two weeks at a time.

4. Share examples of how you practice and live out these training areas.

5. Leaders can form lessons focused on helping small groups learn to go deeper in these training areas.

Group Discussion Points

*   On a scale of 1–10, how focused am I/are we on these one-another actions?

*   What are my/the group's strengths that can help others learn by my/our example?

*   What are my/the group's weaknesses that I/we can learn from another's example?

Imitating
Christlike Empathy

When Jesus saw her weeping, and the Jews who had come along with her also weeping, he was deeply moved in spirit and troubled. "Where have you laid him?" he asked.

"Come and see, Lord," they replied.

Jesus wept.

Then the Jews said, "See how he loved him!"

—John 11:33–36

Background

When we consider John chapter 11's opening, we see our Lord Jesus progress through a difficult situation with some of his closest relationships: Mary, Martha, and their brother Lazarus. Throughout his interactions with the disciples and the family, the Lord shows incredible amounts of empathy, relating to those he loves to the point of acting on their behalf. We have the opportunity to learn and imitate the Lord's empathy in our discipling relationships.

Scriptural Focus

→ Bible study recommended for leader meeting or small group:

- John 11:1–39 – Do we show empathy toward our brothers and sisters when they are having trouble in life or dealing with sin?

One-Another Models

→Consider the following model of how we can transition through the levels of empathy when dealing with one another's challenges:

Figure 2 – The Empathy Pyramid

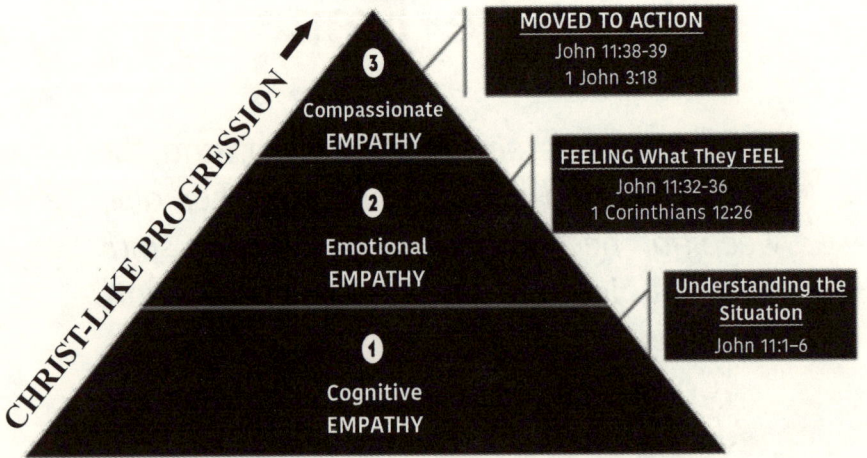

Practical Instruction

1. Identify which level of empathy you embody most.

2. Consider which level of empathy you feel shown the most.

3. Discuss within close relationships ideas of how to grow in compassionate empathy.

4. Discuss within small groups ideas of how to grow in compassionate empathy.

Group Discussion Points

- On a scale of 1–10, how much compassionate empathy is shown within my circle?

- What helps me to show compassionate empathy?

- Who in my circle/small group needs to be shown more empathy?

- Who is a good example in showing compassionate empathy that I can learn from?

Imitating Christlike Mentoring

Follow my example, as I follow the example of Christ.

—1 Corinthians 11:1

Background

When we consider Paul's example of mentoring to Timothy and Titus, his "true sons," we get to see how he both nurtured them and coached them to follow Christ to their best ability. He loved them, and they surely looked up to his example as he followed in the ways of Christ. It seems both Timothy and Titus had a deep trust and respect for Paul's example. That trust and respect allowed Paul to influence them in positive ways that surely promoted stronger relationships in the church bodies where they served. What a blessing to have a mentor you trust help guide you to be your best! Let's strive to mentor others, and let's strive to have mentors for ourselves within the church.

Scriptural Focus

➡ Bible study recommended for leader meeting or small group:

- Philippians 3:17 – Are we investing in mentoring relationships? Humble enough to imitate one another's examples of Christ? (e.g., Timothy ➡ Paul ➡ Christ)
- 2 Timothy 2:1–3 – Do we trust each other to mentor? Are we reliable enough to mentor?
- Titus 2 – What specific character points should we mentor one another in?

One-Another Models

➡ Consider the following model of how to build trust in your mentoring relationships:

Figure 3.1 – Mentoring = [Nurture + Coach] Model

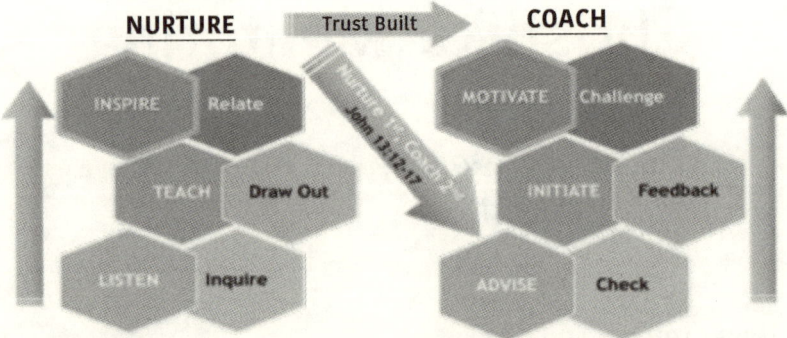

Consider how in John 13:12–17, after Jesus had loved, served, and gained the deep trust of the disciples, he then gave them a lesson and a new challenge for their walk with God.

→Consider the following model of practical mentoring/teaching points found in Titus 2:

Figure 3.2 – Life Stage Group Discipling (Teaching)

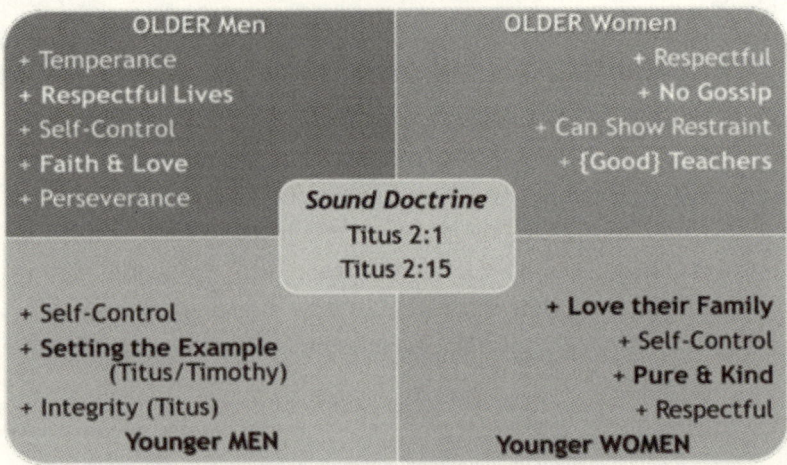

Practical Instruction

1. Based on the life-stage group you best fit in, consider in what areas you are strongest.

2. Consider mentoring a brother or sister in the area in which you are strong to help them in turn develop that strength.

3. Build trust by focusing first on the nurturing steps, then coach at the appropriate time.

4. In the same way, consider in what areas you need the most help.

5. Seek out a mentor whom you trust and respect who is strong in your area of development.

6. Leaders can facilitate mentor-mentee matching by identifying members who would like to be mentors i.e., a mentor pool, mentor groups, etc.

7. Encourage disciples to have multiple mentoring relationships (two or three practically, with a primary mentor for higher levels of vulnerability).

Group Discussion Points

- Does my/our small group have mentoring relationships?

- How could God use me as a mentor to help my sisters and brothers?

- How could God help me by putting a mentor in my life?

- How can we further encourage mentoring relationships in the church?

  - Career/Professional mentoring? Financial mentoring? Marriage/Parenting mentoring? Health and wellness mentoring? Spiritual discipline mentoring?

One-Another New Testament Reference Study

The phrase "one another" is derived from the Greek word *allelon,* which means "one another, each other; mutually, reciprocally."

It occurs **at least N=100 times** in the New Testament.

The Lord Jesus states the golden rule of one another during the Sermon on the Mount (Matthew 7:12). He connects "in everything, do to others what you would have them do to you" as a summation of the Old Testament Law and the Prophets. (Paul echoes this later in Romans 13:8–10.) The Lord further describes a new command to love one another in John chapter 13, and continues to recall it as a central training point for his twelve disciples, especially in his teaching parable of the Vine and the Branches in John chapter 15.

The apostle Paul scribes roughly 60% of these *allelon* occurrences to the Gentile churches.

The apostle John, especially in 1 John chapters 3–4, connects many of these to the greatest commandments of love, #1 and #2.

The apostle Peter teaches that this kind of love is reflected in serving one another and the church as we utilize our God-given gifts to administer his grace (1 Peter 4:7–11).

Approximately N=59 of these *allelon* occurrences are specific commands teaching us how (and how not) to relate to one another. Conviction and obedience to these commands is imperative.

When considering the Great Commission found in Matthew 28, teaching disciples to obey these commands must be a core theme of discipling. These commands form the basis for all Christian relationships, and they have a direct correlation to our evangelism of a lost world (John 13:35). In addition to *allelon,* the Bible uses other words and phrases to instruct us how to relate to others. With that in mind, the following list is not exhaustive, but primarily focuses on the use of *allelon.*

- Love one another. (John 13:34 – This command occurs at least sixteen times.)
- Be devoted to one another. (Romans 12:10)
- Honor one another above yourselves. (Romans 12:10)
- Live in harmony with one another. (Romans 12:16)
- Build one another up. (Romans 14:19; 1 Thessalonians 5:11)
- Have the same attitude of mind toward each other that Jesus had. (Romans 15:5)
- Accept one another. (Romans 15:7)
- Admonish one another. (Romans 15:14; Colossians 3:16)
- Greet one another. (Romans 16:16)
- Care for one another. (1 Corinthians 12:25)
- Serve one another. (Galatians 5:13)
- Bear one another's burdens. (Galatians 6:2)
- Forgive one another. (Ephesians 4:2, 32; Colossians 3:13)
- Be patient with one another. (Ephesians 4:2; Colossians 3:13)
- Speak the truth in love. (Ephesians 4:15, 25)
- Be kind and compassionate to one another. (Ephesians 4:32)
- Speak to one another with psalms, hymns, and spiritual songs. (Ephesians 5:19)
- Submit to one another. (Ephesians 5:21; 1 Peter 5:5)
- Consider others better than yourselves. (Philippians 2:3)
- Look to the interests of one another. (Philippians 2:4)
- Bear with one another. (Colossians 3:13)
- Teach one another. (Colossians 3:16)
- Comfort one another. (1 Thessalonians 4:18 NASB)
- Encourage one another. (1 Thessalonians 5:11)
- Exhort one another. (Hebrews 3:13 NASB)

- Stir up [provoke, stimulate] one another to love and good works. (Hebrews 10:24 ESV)

- Show hospitality to one another. (1 Peter 4:9)

- Employ the gifts that God has given you for the benefit of one another. (1 Peter 4:10)

- Clothe yourselves with humility toward one another. (1 Peter 5:5)

- Pray for one another. (James 5:16)

- Confess your sins to one another. (James 5:16)

- Do not lie to one another. (Colossians 3:9)

- Stop passing judgment on one another. (Romans 14:13)

- If you keep on biting and devouring each other, you'll be destroyed by each other. (Galatians 5:15)

- Let us not become conceited, provoking and envying each other. (Galatians 5:26)

- Do not slander one another. (James 4:11)

- Don't grumble against each other. (James 5:9)

- We do all this because in a real sense "each member belongs to all the others." (Romans 12:5; Ephesians 4:25)